Dick Squires

D1230314

HOW TO PLAY PLATFORM TENNIS

Fourth Revised Edition

McGraw-Hill
perbacks

How to Play
PLATFORM TENNIS

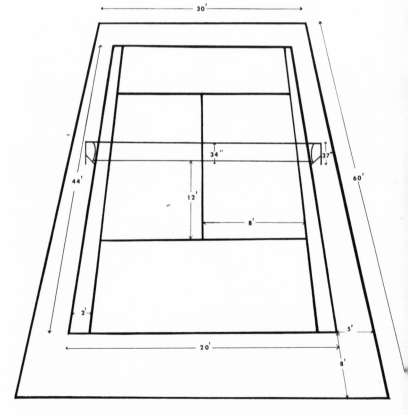

*Dimensions of Platform
Tennis Court Deck*

How to Play
PLATFORM TENNIS

By DICK SQUIRES

Fourth Revised Edition

McGRAW-HILL BOOK COMPANY
New York   St. Louis   San Francisco   Auckland   Bogotá   Düsseldorf
Johannesburg   London   Madrid   Mexico   Montreal   New Delhi
Panama   Paris   São Paulo   Singapore   Sydney   Tokyo   Toronto

First McGraw-Hill Paperback Edition, 1977

1 2 3 4 5 6 7 8 9 0   MU   MU   7 8 3 2 1 0 9 8 7

Reprinted by arrangement with the Devin-Adair Company

Library of Congress Cataloging in Publication Data

Squires, Richard S.
How to play platform tennis.
Reprint of the new rev. ed. published by
Devin-Adair, Old Greenwich, Conn.
1.   Paddle tennis.   I. Title.
GV1006.S734   1977   796.34   77–6820
ISBN 0–07–060530–0

Foreword

This is the first book written on the techniques of playing platform tennis. It is an excellent book, is easy to read, and is liberally sprinkled with photographs illustrating the basics that are discussed.

Dick Squires is a master of many racquet sports and a former National Men's Doubles Champion in platform tennis. As one who himself possesses classic form in all the basic shots—forehand, backhand, serve, overhead, volley, and those wire shots unique to platform tennis—he has succeeded in committing that knowledge to paper for the benefit of the playing public. I believe the book can be fruitfully read not only by newcomers but by experienced players as well.

Platform tennis is the most rapidly growing sport in the United States and in the last few years has begun to find acceptance in several foreign countries. It is expanding not only into new and untraditional venues such as schools and colleges, rooftops in cities, and resorts but also geographically throughout the country. The traditional country club and private court markets also continue to boom. Each year many newcomers are introduced to the game and are "taken" by its unique features, fun, and camaraderie. I consider this book as a major and valuable contribution to the dissemination of knowledge about platform tennis and I recommend it for reading by everyone interested in the game.

Robert A. Brown, Former President
American Platform Tennis Association

The author.

Contents

Author's Note

The thoughts and theories in the following pages are my own, and have been formulated over 25 years of playing most of the racquet games competitively and with a certain degree of success.

The purpose of the book is to put into writing what I know about the wonderful new game of platform tennis. This sport, (and it is a *sport* and not a social gathering) is so new, when compared with other bat and ball games, that, to my knowledge, only two other books have preceded the present one.

While those earlier volumes portrayed the game well, I felt a more in-depth analysis and detailed description of the fundamentals was needed, especially in the areas of shot-making, strategy and strokes. Only a few of the current tennis and squash professionals teach platform tennis, so this book concentrates on these phases of the game.

I have tried to write for *all* players—the seasoned competitor who wishes to raise his game to a higher level, as well as the novice who wants to learn the proper way to play before lapsing into bad habits on his own. The beginner might as well start out correctly, because his improvement then will be that much easier and faster.

D.S.

Introduction:
The Etiquette of the Game

Robert A. Brown

Platform paddle tennis is a keenly competitive sport and one in which by tradition good sportsmanship, integrity, and respect are key elements. It is a game which is played for fun, but there is also an active winter tournament circuit.

The game is played in accordance with the rules of platform tennis as published by the American Platform Tennis Association. For easy reference these are included at the rear of this book. The main purpose of this Introduction, however, is to discuss the *etiquette* of platform tennis play. Etiquette is an area in which, unlike rules which are generally more specific, there may be differences of opinion, or judgment may have to be exercised. Since platform tennis is one of the most rapidly growing sports in the country and is attracting many new participants, the APTA believes it desirable to provide these guidelines on the etiquette of the game. In doing so, it is recognized that "etiquette" does have its "gray areas." Therefore these comments are offered, not as hard and fast rules, but as suggested guidelines of behavior. In any case, it is hoped that the tradition of the game will be maintained through a continued high degree of sportsmanship and mutual respect and that this introductory chapter may assist in furthering that tradition by offering worthwhile suggestions on personal behavior while playing this rewarding game.

FOOTFAULT

The footfault is the area in which the greatest amount of self-control is required by the player. Seldom will fellow players advise another player that he is footfaulting for fear of "offending." Yet if, in serving, he is stepping on or over the baseline before striking the ball, he is breaking the rules just as seriously as if he faults on the serve by hitting it into the net, or out. The fact is that players may not know they are footfaulting. This is because, in serving, many players make a slight movement of the forward foot, which is legal, but in doing so they step on or over the line. A player can find out if he is footfaulting by asking a fellow player to observe his serve. Conversely, a polite comment to another player, who himself will not ask, may not be out of order. One subtle way to handle this is to ask a player if he would like to have you call his footfaults during his practice serves.

Other than the above suggestions, it has become generally accepted etiquette not to call the opposing server on footfaults during either a friendly or tournament game which does not have linesmen. The server is "on his honor" not to footfault; therefore all players should exercise the self-control necessary to stay behind the line while serving. Apart from the rule-breaking and etiquette aspects of footfaulting, linesmen will call footfaults in the semi-finals and finals of major tournaments and any player who is in the habit of footfaulting regularly may have a difficult time adjusting to a correct service procedure under the pressure of tournament competition. The usual result is that he will lose points on called footfaults or serve a higher percentage of faults in trying to adjust to a legal service.

So, in this area above all others, etiquette says that players must exercise the greatest degree of self-control in order not to break the rules and/or offend others. Practice serving legally, and check with others by asking that your service be watched.

LINE CALLS

In most tournaments, lines will be called by linesmen in the semi-finals and finals. In tournament rounds prior to that and in other friendly games where there are no linesmen, the general rule is that all lines are called by the receiving team, i.e. you call lines on your side, the opponents call lines on their side. Each side should, obviously, call the ball in or out honestly and without regard to the play situation. The decision of the team whose responsibility it is to make the call is final. The following refinements are suggested:

1. If an "out" call is not promptly made, the ball is considered "in" and play should continue.

2. On receipt of service, the receiver's partner should call the deep service line and the center line. The receiver should call the wide serve on the outside line. The receiver's partner may do so also.

3. If a member of the receiving team makes an "out" call but his partner thinks the ball was in, a "let" should be played.

4. A certain (hopefully minimum) amount of friendly kidding about opponents' line calls is inevitable. But etiquette dictates that the opponents' line calls are to be respected and considered final. In the end, the balance of "questionable" calls will usually balance off between the two sides.

"LET" BALL ON SERVICE

The server's partner is closest to the net and in the best position to hear a "let." He should call it promptly, loud and clear. It is also permissible for either member of the receiving team, if he believes he heard the ball tick the net, to promptly call a "let," in which case the service should be played again.

BALL HITTING PLAYER

If a ball touches any part of a player's body (including any part of the hand) either before landing or hitting the screen on the player's side or after landing fairly in the court, it results in loss of point. Even if the player is standing outside the boundaries of the court, the point is lost if the ball strikes him before landing on the deck or hitting a screen. Often a ball striking a player just barely grazes his clothing or hair. It is good etiquette for the player himself to declare that the ball touched him and award the point to the opponents. It is not good etiquette for any player to accuse or declare categorically that the ball hit an opponent and thereby "claim" the point. He may, if he wishes, politely ask if it did, but the determination of whether or not the ball hit the player is that player's to make, and his integrity and decision in the matter should be accepted.

THE "TICK"

A ball which is "ticked" is barely grazed with the paddle, and often when this happens only the player who "ticks" the ball can hear or feel it. It is good etiquette for the player doing so to promptly declare that he touched the ball and award the point to the opponents. It is poor etiquette for opponents to declare that a player "ticked" the ball and claim the point. The best person to determine whether the ball was ticked is the player himself and it is good etiquette to respect his integrity and decision.

TOUCHING THE NET

Touching the net with any part of the body or the paddle during play is loss of point. A player touching the net should promptly declare that he did so and award the point to the opponents.

THE "CARRY"

The "carry" is difficult to define, but the word fairly suggests what occurs, and it is illegal. It is an excessively long contact between the paddle and the ball, as distinct from a cleanly struck shot. The carry is illegal because, if practiced, it could give a player an unfair advantage. The carry can inadvertently occur in almost any playing situation, but one of the most common is when two teams are having a rapid exchange of volleys near the net and a player, in moving backward while receiving and attempting to return a shot, unintentionally "catches" or "cradles" the ball on his racket. If in his judgment he has "carried" the ball he should so declare it and award the point to opponents. A "double hit" can also occur in this situation and in the more difficult wire shots. This is a version of the "carry" wherein the player in attempting to return a shot hits the ball twice in quick succession. It is rare but it does happen. And since it is illegal it should be promptly declared by the player and the point awarded to the opponents.

RETURN THE BALL TO THE SERVER

When a point is completed, if the ball is lying on your side of the court and your opponent is serving, it is good etiquette to pick up the ball and either give it to your opponent's net man who can give it to the server, or gently bounce the ball to the server in his next service position, waiting a moment if his back is turned before "feeding" it to him. All too often players simply kick or push the ball in the opponents' direction or arbitrarily hit the ball just anywhere over to the other side. This makes the server walk around chasing the ball, it is discourteous, and it results in a slow-moving game. It is good etiquette to do your part by picking up the ball and getting it to the server in an easy and accommodating manner. If everyone does this it will be easier on you when your turn comes to serve! And finally, above all, resist the temptation of venting aggravation at missing an easy shot by ferociously slamming the ball about the court after the point is lost.

THE LADY IN MIXED DOUBLES

This can be a sensitive subject. However no document on etiquette would be complete without touching at least briefly on the subject. Specifically the question is how the man should play against the lady in an opposing mixed doubles team, particularly if the lady is the weaker of the two partners. There are two schools of thought. The first, which is more often applied in friendly games, says that the man should be "gentlemanly" by not driving the ball hard at the lady at net or in returning her serve and should not work her corner disproportionately. This does have the advantage of balancing play between opposing partners, it is "gentlemanly," and it avoids the label of "picking on the lady." In an otherwise close contest it can also lead to losing the match. The other school of thought says that a team is a team, sex makes no difference and the normal strategy to beat a team which may be unbalanced is to play the weaker partner. If that partner happens to be a lady, so be it. And if the lady does not like that, she need not play (or can get better). Both viewpoints have merit and both have their strong advocates. It is not uncommon to see a "double standard" practiced, with the first school of thought being applied in friendly, social games where winning or losing may be unimportant or even in an unbalanced tournament match; and the second standard being applied in a keenly contested tournament match. We believe it best to leave this choice to one's personal discretion.

PUNCTUALITY

Platform paddle tennis is a doubles game requiring four players. It is good etiquette to be on time for a pre-arranged game and not inconvenience the other players by being late.

A Word about
Right and Left Hands

In all cases, unless otherwise noted, the text dealing with the basic strokes is written for a right-handed platform tennis player. A southpaw will have to keep this in mind as he reads and attempts to follow and practice the principles suggested in this book.

It has also been assumed that the readers' opponents are right-handed.

Because of the increasing number of "lefties" playing the game, however, a few comments have been included specifically for their benefit.

Finally, when describing the left side or right side of a court, I am referring to that side as seen from *across the net*. In other words, the left side of the opposition's court is the forehand side and the right court is the backhand side.

D.S.

CHAPTER 1

A Short History
of the Game

While games such as tennis and squash have foreign roots (England), and are over 100 years old, our favorite sport, a stepchild of tennis and squash, goes back a mere 49 years, and its birthplace is as American as apple pie and baseball.

During the winter of 1928 a handful of tennis-minded businessmen in Scarsdale, New York decided to build an all-purpose deck above the snow level that would offer them a weekend playing field during the dreary, cold months.

Originally this platform was erected for the purpose of deck tennis, volley-ball and badminton. Fessenden Blanchard joined his good friend, James K. Cogswell, in building it in the latter's backyard. By the end of that winter other members of the so-called Old Army Athletes joined in on the work and fun. The name of the group does not imply that they were Civil War veterans. Jim Cogswell's home was located on historic Old Army Road. Upon completion of the deck, eight foot high chicken mesh screening was installed around the court to keep the balls in the playing area and the dogs out.

One Sunday morning Cogswell showed up with some paddles and sponge rubber balls that were being used for a game played on the sidewalks and playgrounds of New York City called "Paddle Tennis." The paddle was square, had no holes, and was light weight. With these rather crude implements they began playing a game utilizing the same rules as regular lawn tennis. They very quickly forgot other sports since the playing deck proved to be perfectly suited for a bat and ball game.

Because the deck approximated one half of the area of a tennis court, they quickly discovered (as do all newcomers to platform tennis) that the rallies were extended, and the activity in such a confined area was a great deal of frantic fun, plus wonderful exercise.

The story goes that one day a ball during a rally hit into the large-mesh screening after bouncing fairly in the court and stuck there. Blanchard ran outside and smacked the ball with the paddle. It dislodged and soared across the net between his opponents. Thus the game's unique characteristic of playing "off the wires" was born, and as is so often the case, by a freak accident. Right then and there they decided that the ball was in play if it bounced into the screening, as long as it could be returned before it had struck twice on the deck.

During that winter they began to add other rules. For example, they decided to allow only one service, thus eliminating the tremendous advantage a strong server has. This also speeded up the play.

Friends and neighbors dropped by to see them play and to learn this "bastard form" of tennis, and many a pleasant day of exhilarating exercise resulted. Many wives were quick to join in, perhaps because they discovered they could spend extra hours with their husbands over the weekends, but they too soon became proficient.

Being gregarious people, the avid inventors of platform tennis told their friends and associates of their new game. They erected a new deck at the Cogswells', and the playing area of the court was reduced slightly to 60' x 30' with the lines 44' x 20', which is the same as badminton. The back and side wires were raised from eight to ten feet and eventually to the present height of twelve feet.

Most of the Old Army Athletes were members of the Fox Meadow Tennis Club, a mile away from the Cogswells' residence. In 1931, they approached the Board at the club and after much debate between the tennis players and the platform tennis players, it was decided that a platform tennis court should be built.

The tennis playing members acquiesced after it was agreed that a backboard could be erected at one end of the court to allow for tennis practice. A special winter membership was offered, so that the club could stay open all year round. The first club course was built at Fox Meadow in November of 1931 for the reasonable price of approximately $400.

By then the rules had been fairly well established, as were the dimensions. Donald K. Evans engineered and redesigned the backstop and screening, so that the problem of irregular bounces off the screen was, for the most part, solved. This was a key innovation.

By the end of 1931 over 20 private playing decks had been built according to the plans drawn up by Blanchard. There is no question that the Old Army Athletes did a great job of selling their new found love. The first platform tennis tournament on record was held in Scarsdale in December 1931. Forty-two teams competed in the championship which was won by Fessenden Blanchard and Earle Gatchell, defeating Randolph Compton and James Hynson.

As a result of the year-round activity, Fox Meadow began to prosper, with many new individuals joining the club specifically to play the new game. The first decks erected at a few of the clubs were built right on top of the tennis courts and were portable. As the game grew, however, and became more popular, permanent courts were erected in open, unutilized areas.

It was only a question of time before adjoining communities heard of the new winter, outdoor, bat and ball game being played in Scarsdale. The Manursing Island Club in Rye, New York, had some addicts, and in 1932 two courts were erected. Jim Hynson, Perce Fuller, Ken Ward, John Stephenson and Jack Ten Eyck were all instrumental in bringing about the installation of these platforms. A friendly, but intense rivalry began between the two clubs and inter-club competition was born. Sand was added in the paint for sure-footing in 1934-35, which helped facilitate playing even in the most abominable weather.

The American Paddle Tennis Association was organized in

1934 and Fessenden Blanchard became its first president. The name of the Association as well as the sport (though most players still call it "paddle tennis") was formally and officially changed in 1950 to American Platform Tennis Association.

In 1935, the first "national" championships were organized and held at Fox Meadow. Men's singles, men's and women's doubles and mixed doubles were staged. Singles was dropped after only three years because the game proved far more suited for doubles play. Ed Grafmueller won the first two years and Charlie O'Hearn the third.

The game rapidly spread to Connecticut and New Jersey, and in 1936 a couple of New Jersey upstarts, Harold Holmes and Dick Newell, walked off with the national doubles crown, defeating Blanchard and Gatchell in five sets.

By 1940, just prior to World War II, platform tennis was being played quite extensively in Scarsdale, Rye, South Orange, and Englewood, New Jersey, Hartford and Greenwich, Connecticut. The popularity of the game spread by word of mouth since little or no publicity or promotion was sought by the inventors of the sport.

In 1939, there were 15 member clubs in the APTA. Even though gas rationing slowed down the growth of the game during the war, the men who stayed at home saved their coupons and were able to practice on weekends. The women's and mixed doubles national championships were discontinued between 1943 and 1945 because of wartime travel difficulties, but the men's doubles title was played each and every year.

By 1954, 23 clubs became members of the APTA, and later the number was augmented to 37. In 1963 there were 70 member clubs and today there are over 250 plus some 40 individual memberships. It has been estimated that the game is growing at the rate of some 25% each year, which certainly makes platform tennis one of the fastest growing racquet and ball games in America.

Why the meteoric growth of interest and participation? Apparently there are many people who feel the same need for outdoor winter exercise as did the Old Army Athletes. There have also been many "sick clubs" during and after the Depression that needed the financial resuscitation that a year-round sport offered. For an active businessman or harassed housewife, the game offers a release—vigorous, relaxing activity, demanding little time and money.

The same convivial spirit and enthusiasm so evident on the original court prevails today. The rugged exercise and stiff competition are always counterbalanced with the post-game social amenities. We all hope that as the game continues to grow this feeling of camaraderie between competitors and lasting friendships between partners will endure.

And certainly the game will continue to grow. The APTA has sent court plans to such foreign countries as Belgium, France, Canada, England, Russia, Australia, Italy and Poland. Some of these countries will build courts and become smitten with the game. In the not too distant future perhaps we will find ourselves in world-wide competition, battling for an impressive piece of silver which will be emblematic of international supremacy.

Armed forces service stations located in colder climes represent a sizable area for expansion. Ski resorts, golf clubs, city playgrounds, schools and colleges, all are untapped markets for the introduction of platform tennis.

The original two founders of this marvelous game have, regrettably, passed on. Not a splinter is left of the original deck, but the game is very much alive and growing. It will not be too many more years before qualifying rounds will be necessary in order to compete in national championships.

CHAPTER 2

The Ground Strokes

As in all racquet and ball sports, you will see a few very good players in platform tennis who hit the ball in an unorthodox manner. Some of them use jerky strokes and employ an excessive amount of top spin. Others slice practically all of their shots. A few hold the paddle like a ping pong bat. These players, however, are the exception and not the rule. The old adage that states: "The proper way is always the easiest and best way" very much holds true in this game.

If you have played any tennis at all, you should have little trouble hitting platform tennis ground strokes. Just keep in mind that the court is approximately half the size of a tennis court; therefore, it is *not* necessary to hit a long, flowing stroke. In addition, obtaining consistent depth on your ground strokes (which one strives for in tennis) is not only unnecessary, but undesirable, because of that great equalizer, the back screen.

So, while the fundamental forehand and backhand strokes are similar to tennis, by necessity your swing will be shorter, somewhat faster, and the ball hit with an abbreviated follow-through.

No mention will be made of hitting *flat* ground strokes. The court is just too small, the net too high, the baseline too short, and the playing area too confined to permit you to hit flat shots with any kind of regularity. Of paramount importance is consistency, and this steadiness can only be realized by using *controlled spin* when hitting ground strokes.

1. *Forehand:* The so-called Eastern Grip is the most widely

used and accepted way of holding the paddle. Take the paddle, hold the playing surface vertical to the ground and merely shake hands with the handle.

Forehand Grip

The moment your opponent hits a shot in the direction of your forehand start your paddle up and back immediately, but slowly. Starting your backswing early will preclude the necessity of a last second wind-up and a fast "flick" stroke. All your ground strokes should be hit as smoothly and as effortlessly as possible. Attempt to time your backswing so that you are taking your paddle back at the same pace as the ball is travelling on its way to you. This will help your timing and overall rhythm.

From backswing to follow-through the movement of the paddle should be *continuous and fluid.*

It is important to turn sideways (when you have the time) and step forward as your paddle meets the ball. As with *all* the basic strokes, you should have your body *weight,* not merely your arm, behind your shot. Everything moving forward, or in the direction of your shot, will help to groove your stroke, and will also put far more "sting" or pace on the ball.

a) *Top Spin Forehand:* As your paddle makes contact with the ball, roll your entire forearm slightly (keeping the wrist stiff). This will cause the paddle to "cover" the ball, so to speak, and you have applied controlled top spin. This top spin will help to keep the ball low and in the court. In time you will "feel" exactly how much spin is required to gain the desired control and pace, with confidence.

Your follow-through should be out in front and following the flight of the ball. It is not as pronounced or as long a stroke as in

John Mangan shows why he has one of the most devastating top spin forehands in the game. Again, the weight is on the foot closest to the net, and the follow-through is high and closed, indicating that he has applied top spin to the ball.

tennis. Remember, the ball will go where your racquet head guides it, so make your follow-through precisely to the spot where you intend to hit the ball.

In addition, the follow-through must be higher than the height of the net, or chances are the ball will go into the net and you have lost the point on an error.

b) *Slice Forehand:* On the slice forehand, your paddle contacts the ball on the *underside* and back spin (as against top spin) is thereby applied.

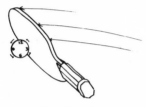

Forehand Top Spin

Forehand Slice

The slice forehand is usually employed as a defensive return— when you are chasing after a ball and do not have time to get set and really "whack it." A ball that bounces high will also have to be hit with a slicing motion. The slice forehand can, however, also be used effectively as a change of pace in order to surprise your opponents with an unexpected bounce.

As mentioned earlier the top spin forehand is hit with a "closed" paddle, whereas the slice forehand calls for an "open" paddle with the playing surface facing upward at approximately a 45-degree angle from the plane of the deck.

Unlike the top spin shot, you will use a snap of the wrist to impart the "cut" underspin to the ball. Actually this stroke is hit quite similarly to the volley, with perhaps even more of an exaggerated "bite."

Slicing down on the ball also helps you keep the ball low, so that your opponents will have to hit up in order to make their return.

2. *Backhand:* The backhand is also hit very much like its counterpart in tennis, except, again, the swing is somewhat

shorter. The grip, as in tennis, is a quarter of a turn (clockwise) of the paddle away from the forehand.

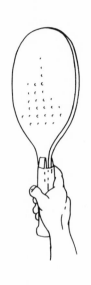

Backhand Grip

The instant the ball leaves the opponent's paddle and heads toward your backhand side (just as for all ground strokes), start taking your paddle *up and back*. This will prevent you from rushing your stroke. Many players are a fraction of a second late on their ground strokes due to a last-minute backswing.

It is even more important on the backhand ground stroke (than on the forehand) to *turn sideways,* and to step into the ball as you make your stroke. When you turn sideways, it is not a closed stance with the right foot crossed over toward the alley. It is a sideways stance with the right foot stepping *toward the net*. It is easier for most players to obtain much more natural power on the forehand, so in order to compensate and to add pace to your backhand, you must have your body weight moving into the ball as you hit.

The backhand should be hit about three to six inches *in front of* your right toe (the forehand is hit approximately by your left heel). The paddle head at the moment of impact should be higher than the wrist. Keep your elbow tucked in next to your body; don't allow it to lead your racquet!

a) *Top Spin Backhand:* On only rare occasions will you have enough time to hit a top spin backhand. The time to hit over the ball and apply top spin to your backhand is when your opponents hit a soft shot that "sits up" and allows you to come in and "spank it."

To hit the occasional top spin backhand, start with the paddle *below* the level of the ball, with your paddle face open. Then

Gordon Gray, three-time National Mixed Doubles Champion and also National Men's Doubles Winner with Jesse Sammis III, showing classic form as he returns a backhand. Note the weight on his forward foot, the body sideways to the net and his eye on the ball.

come over the ball with the roll of your wrist. The follow-through, again, is up and out over the top of the net.

b) *Slice Backhand:* Because of the lack of time, most of the better players have developed a *hard* slice backhand shot, which provides speed and control and a ball with a low trajectory. There is a safety margin in this stroke and, if grooved low, you will be able to compensate for the loss of power obtainable with a top spin backhand.

When hitting this shot, the paddle head starts from a position higher than the ball (just the reverse of top spin), then sweeps through on an oblique angle, contacting the side and underneath part of the ball with the open face of the paddle. The cocked wrist, with the paddle still open, snaps through at or just above the height of the net, and, of course, in the direction you want to place the ball.

Probably 90% of your backhands will and should be hit with controlled slice rather than top spin, so, again, practice, practice, practice!

GROUND STROKES RECAP:

1. Forehand and backhand strokes in platform tennis are similar to tennis, with the exception of a *shorter, faster* swing and an *abbreviated follow-through*.

2. *Consistency* and *steadiness* rather than overwhelming power are the keys to platform tennis ground strokes.

3. Start your backswing in plenty of time.

4. Turn *sideways,* whenever possible, on all ground strokes, and *bend your knees* on all low balls.

5. Whenever possible, *step into* the ball.

6. There are basically two (2) types of ground strokes, *top spin* and *slice*.

CHAPTER 3

The Service

Developing a *dependable* service is perhaps even more important than ultimately developing an effective or offensive one. After all, you are only allowed one serve, which, incidentally, makes American platform tennis unique in the world of racquet games that employ overhand serves. Lawn tennis, squash racquets, squash tennis, court tennis, hard racquets, all allow the luxury of two services. In addition, placing the ball in the proper service area is easier in those sports.

It is not unusual for even the very best platform tennis players to "choke up" on their serves in crucial games—sometimes to the point where two, three and even four balls in a row fail to find their mark in the opponents' service courts. Such a collapse can, needless to say, completely shatter the confidence of a player and have disastrous effects on the rest of his game—not to mention his partner's.

So, first and foremost, is the absolute necessity for developing a *consistent* service with which you feel comfortable and confident. Many players have actually used a reliable *underhand* slice serve to be doubly certain the ball is put in play, but this is a last resort.

The safest service is, therefore, one in which you can "feel" the control of the ball on your paddle. Opening up, or laying back the racquet face slightly (which means employing more of a backhand grip than a forehand) will help your control immeasurably.

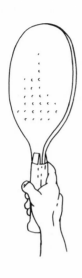

Service Grip

Don't be concerned about the lack of speed at first, since a hard-hit clean "ace" in platform tennis is practically as rare as a no-hitter in baseball.

Even if you are a novice, you should start out with a modified *spin* service, rather than be content to push the ball in play off a flat paddle head. Eventually you will by playing and practicing develop an effective service with a spin. On the other hand, you will show very little or no improvement if you continue to hit your service with a flat paddle. The rest of your game will develop, but the very important service stroke will retard your overall effectiveness and progress as a player unless you get off to a good start in developing a reliable, controlled spin service.

Basically, the platform tennis service is a shorter, abbreviated version of the classic lawn tennis stroke; everything is more restrained and contained. After all, with only one service you cannot just lean back and let go.

The proper starting position is with the paddle and ball touching together and out in front of you at approximately eye level. Your body should face sideways to the net with the weight resting comfortably on the back foot. The front foot should be placed within one or two inches of the baseline in order to prevent footfaulting (stepping on or over the back line prior to hitting the ball). The feet should be so aligned that if someone took a straight stick and placed it in front of the tips of your sneakers it would point precisely to the direction of the court in which you are serving.

Stand approximately 12 to 15 inches to the right or left of the center, so that your approach to the net behind your serve is on

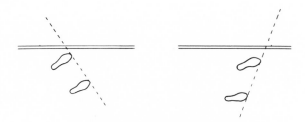

Foot positions when serving to
deuce and ad court

an angle. This position will help reduce the angle of your opponents' returns.

There are two schools of thought regarding the initial stage of the service. One theory states you should merely pull your paddle directly back to the cocked position behind your head and then make your toss-up of the ball. The other theory, which I personally recommend, is that the paddle and the ball should be pulled down simultaneously by merely dropping your two hands. There is absolutely no work involved in this first step—as a matter of fact, it helps to keep you relaxed and your service swing grooved. Also by employing this "sweeping" windup you are building up a certain degree of momentum.

At a comfortable point just above the kneecaps the hand holding the paddle will almost automatically and effortlessly continue on back to a position approximately level with the right ear. The wrist is cocked up and back. As the paddle and ball are brought downward, the body weight begins to shift from the back foot toward the front.

At the same time you make the all-important, precise toss-up. When you toss the ball in the air be sure to keep your head up. Some players make the mistake of throwing the ball up, and then looking to see where it is going. Golfers have to keep their heads down; platform tennis servers must keep their heads up!

Having all your weight now on the forward foot helps you to obtain a little pace on the ball. Also, by falling forward, you gain a few extra valuable steps on your way to the net behind your service. *And you must always go to net behind your service.*

You should reach up and strike the ball at the *apex* of the toss-up. Your right arm should not be bent, but fully extended at the moment of impact. As a matter of fact, your entire body should be stretched to its full length since attaining the maximum height will help you to put the ball in your opponent's court. Employing the semi-open (or toward the backhand) grip will help you "bite" or "cover" the ball with the paddle. The spin is applied by snapping your wrist forward at the instant of impact.

There are actually two types of spin services you should attempt and, eventually, master. Both are hit with the "open" paddle face and with a snap of the wrist.

The "twist" service is usually employed when you are trying to place the ball to your opponent's *backhand*. To twist a service, your racquet head should make contact with the ball at the top and slightly to the *left* side of the ball.

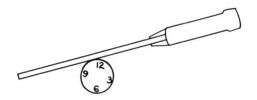

Twist Service

The ball is tossed slightly behind the head, so that your back has to arch prior to hitting it. This gives the ball some top, as well as reverse spin that causes it to bounce to the right, or toward your opponent's backhand side.

It is well to add here that you cannot, and should not, expect to obtain as much "bite" or spin on the ball using a wooden platform tennis paddle as is possible with a lawn tennis racquet strung with gut. The smooth, sponge rubber ball just cannot be "grabbed" by the even, solid surface of your bat.

The "side spin" serve is used when you wish to put the ball wide to your adversary's forehand. The toss-up for this service is usually thrown slightly off to the right of your normal toss-up. This will help you to come across the ball which, in turn, will give a wider angle of trajectory. By contacting the ball on the right side you will keep the ball spinning away from your opponent's forehand, or to the left, after it lands in his service court.

If the very top of the ball be considered as 12 o'clock, the twist service is hit at approximately 11 o'clock and the slice service at 3 o'clock.

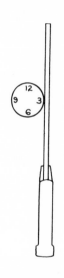

Slice Service

The follow-through is just as important as the other parts of the service; *i.e.,* the wind-up, toss-up, and impact. You must follow through *completely* to your left side in order to make certain that everything you have put into the serve stays in. That is to say, not following through on the service is the same as a boxer winding up from the floor for a big knockout punch, then ending up with a jab that travels no more than 2 inches. What a waste of potential power and style! What a superfluous amount of excessive work and needless energy! In addition, you are actually doing extra work if you fail to follow through to the left side. It takes a great amount of effort to stop that 14-ounce paddle from going all the way through naturally after making contact with the ball.

So, first and foremost, get the ball into play on your service Then develop the confidence to *place* the ball where you want it to go. The mighty "cannon ball" service is out of the question. As a matter of fact, a hard-smashed service is undesirable since your opponents can take it off the back screen and slam it at or through you.

The second important single attribute of an effective platform tennis serve is to *move your opponent*. Do not allow him the luxury of planting his feet and walloping his return of service at you. Keep him off balance, and don't always serve to the same place. Prevent your opponent from anticipating where you are going to put it by serving to different spots.

The majority of your serves, however, should be aimed at your opponents' *weak* side, and it should not take too many serves for you to discover from which side he prefers to return the ball—forehand or backhand.

In addition, occasionally a service *right at* your opponent pays dividends—as when a pitcher in baseball "jams" the batter. Serving straight at an opponent also prevents him from getting off a wide angle return.

As mentioned previously the limiting factor of having only one serve can be rather awesome, especially during the key games in competition. If you feel a "creeping tightness" coming over you, it will help immensely to pause, take a few deep breaths, and toe the line for a deliberate second or two prior to serving. It will help you relax.

No matter how much confidence you might develop in your service, be sure *always* to take at least two practice serves into both the forehand and backhand courts prior to serving "for real."

Also make certain the last practice service goes in. If all your practice serves are faults, keep making them until you get one in. Don't handicap yourself on your first "for real" service by having to adjust in order to get the ball in play. In other words, have a "feel" of the ball on the paddle prior to actually starting.

Many even of the best players have developed a bad habit when playing just for fun. When their turn comes to serve, they take a few practice shots, and then say, "First one in." This is not only unfair to the receiver, since all the pressure is off the server, but it can cause problems when the server has to serve under the pressure of competition.

When practicing, therefore, you should simulate tournament conditions. Otherwise you will discover the pressure is much worse when you become involved in competition, and chances are

Herb FitzGibbon, National Men's Doubles champion (1974 with John Beck), has one of the most effective and consistent serves in the game. Note the fully extended arm, and that both feet are off the deck to attain the maximum height.

you will have more of a tendency to "choke" or "clutch" on those first few serves.

SERVICE RECAP:

1. You are only allowed *one* serve.

2. *First* and foremost, *put the ball in play.*

3. *Second,* develop a *controlled* spin (twist or side spin) service.

4. Then, and only then, work on *placing* the ball, and hitting it *deep* into your opponent's court.

5. Keep your opponents off-balance by *moving* the served ball to various spots.

6. Attempt to serve to your opponents' *weakness.*

7. *Always* go to net behind your serve.

8. Take a minimum of four practice serves.

CHAPTER 4

The Return of Service

Return of service is perhaps the only stroke hit off of your opponent's shot that frequently allows you the luxury of time to turn sideways, anchor your feet, wind up and smash the ball *offensively*. If the service is not hit well, or properly placed, you will have the opportunity and time to step in and really crush the ball—often for a winner or a forced error.

About the most important elements to keep in mind when hitting your return of serve are to catch the ball on the *rise* (right after it bounces), to *move into the ball,* and to have your *body weight shifting forward* in the direction of your shot the moment your paddle meets the ball. This will help you to obtain greater pace to your return and it also puts more pressure on the server as he races to net for his important return-of-service volley. For a split second your opponent might believe you are coming all the way in behind your return (blitzing) and, perhaps, he will be more prone to rush his volley. Or he might even take his eye off the ball to ascertain your intentions. At any rate, there are many good reasons to catch the service on the rise and be moving into the shot as you make your return.

Another fundamental part of this stroke is to start your backswing the instant the server strikes the ball. This will keep you from rushing your shot and from taking a last-second "flick" at the ball.

You should stand as far in as your opponent's service will allow you. The better his serve, the farther back (toward the base line) you will be compelled to take position. The weaker his

The author has caught the ball on the rise and his follow-through is out in front and aimed at the top of the net. Note how he is moving in on the ball. The position of the paddle indicates he has applied top spin.

serve, the closer you can stand toward the net. Whenever possible, try to position yourself no farther back than just *inside* the baseline.

While you are waiting for your opponent to serve to you, assume a semi-crouched position, bend over slightly from the hips and lean forward with your body facing the net. Your feet should be spread comfortably apart, weight forward on the soles of your sneakers, the knees slightly bent and never stiff, and your paddle pointing more or less in the direction of the net. The paddle head should be up rather than down and out in front of you in a position from which you can hit either a backhand or a forehand return at will. This is the "ready" position, and you are prepared to move quickly in any direction once your opponent serves. Generally speaking, the waiting or ready position in platform tennis is the typical athlete's stance—one which helps the hitter to move quickly and cat-like in any direction.

The return of service is the *second* most important stroke; only the service takes priority. As with other platform tennis shots, the key is *consistency*. No matter what shot you attempt, do whatever is necessary to be sure the ball clears the net. (It is always better to hit out of court on your errors than into the net). First and foremost, therefore, your return of service *must* be returned.

While you are returning, you should concentrate solely on watching the ball come off your opponent's racquet. Your eyes, your mind, and your total concentration should be zeroed in on that ball and where you plan to hit it. If the service pulls you wide, or comes right at you, you will not have time to think about what to do with the ball. Your movement and return will have to be accomplished instinctively. This instinct can be developed with play and practice.

When making the return of service, the same axiom for all platform tennis strokes holds true: *mix up* your shots as much as possible. Unless you discover on obvious defensive or offensive weakness in your opponents' play (for examples, the man at net is afraid of a ball hit right at him, or the service is very weak, which provides you with the opportunity to make a "kill" practically every time), try to hit a *different* return every time. Again, keep your opponents off-balance, wary and worried. Do not ever let them know what or where your next return will be.

The best and most logical "bread and butter" return of service is hit fairly *hard and low,* straight down the *middle.* The net man on the other side of the court will not be able to "poach" (cross over and cut your ball off with a volley) and the incoming server will have to "dig" in order to make an effective return volley. Always remember the age-old center theory: "The safest and most effectual place to hit the ball when your opponents have the net is down the middle, between them."

An effective variation on the return of service is the "dink." This is a very short, soft, sharply angled cross court that just barely clears the top of the net. It will draw your opponent (the incoming server) very wide and away from the center. If he is ambling in, rather than charging, you might very well catch him in an awkward position where he is compelled to half volley or make a weak volley that "sits up." This return also draws him away from protecting the center and your next return should be down the middle.

Another return of service is a very hard hit shot aimed right *at* the opposing net man. If he is at all jittery about being at net, a well-aimed forehand lashed right at him or down his alley will do wonders to further undermine his confidence. This shot will also "keep him honest"; he will not be too apt to poach since you have made him aware you can hit "down the line" as well as cross court.

A lob return placed deftly over the head of the opposing net man is another variation of the return of service that will keep the serving team off-balance.

It is important to analyze your opponents' serves, as well as how they come to net behind them. Do they move the service around to different spots? Can they place it to your backhand, or do they invariably serve to your forehand? Do they come to net slowly or do they charge in like a rhino? Does the net man attempt to move out and cut off your cross court returns, or is he fairly content to stay on his side of the court? How close does the net man stand to the net? Is he vulnerable for a lob or a smashing forehand aimed at his chest? In other words, study your opponents carefully and vary your return of service accordingly.

Above all, remember that this particular stroke is called the "*Return* of Service." Consistency of return will bring far more dividends than successfully making one in five sensational, hard-hit shots down the opponent's alley.

RETURN OF SERVICE RECAP:

1.   This is one of the few shots in platform tennis that affords you the *time* to wind up and hit a powerful, *offensive* shot.

2.   Stand in as *close* to your *service line* as the opponents' serves allow, catch the ball *on the rise*, and *move into* the ball as you hit.

3.   *Consistency* is the key aim when making this stroke.

4.   *Mix up* your returns as much as possible.

5.   Various returns—
   a) Low and down the middle.
   b) Hard at the opposing net man.
   c) Lob over opposing net man's head.
   d) A wide-angled, soft and low "dink."

CHAPTER 5

Blitzing

"Blitzing" or going in behind a good, low return of service is a tactic which, if done well, will win many points. Unlike lawn tennis where it is very important for a doubles team to go up or be back together, in platform tennis your partner should stay back to protect you in case your return of service sits up and allows your opponents to volley the ball at, or past you.

This is probably the only instance in *any* doubles racquets game where the so-called "I" formation (your partner directly behind you) can pay off.

When you start in behind your return, your partner should leave his side of the court and move over toward the middle of the base line in order to protect you. This position will enable him to cover the court better if a ball is hit by you.

Obviously you will be compelled to return to the base line as quickly as possible if your "mission" fails because of a poor return of service. Your partner, therefore, would most likely be very smart (depending upon how much trouble you are in) to lob, thus giving you more time to retreat to the base line.

On the other hand, if your return is a good one, low and hard, then your opponent is compelled to volley up. By going in behind your shot you will be in an excellent position to "powder" the ball for a winner. The best place to volley is *between* the opposing players or right at them. Be sure not to hit your volley too hard, as the opposition will undoubtedly be retreating anyhow, and you do not want your ball to come off the back screen.

Blitzing is a relatively new tactic, one that has only been employed during the past few years. It can, if done well, win many points.

BLITZING RECAP:

1. *Go in* behind a hard, low return of service.

2. Your partner *stays back* and covers the entire back court, thereby offering you protection.

3. Your logical place for a putaway volley is *between* or *right at* your opponents, but not too hard.

Gordon Gray has hit a hard, low forehand return of service and is charging in behind his shot hoping to volley his opponent's return away for a winner. His partner, Jesse Sammis, has moved over toward the center of the back court to cover for Gray should the opposition hit one through him.

CHAPTER 6

Screen Play

Playing the ball off the wire, side and/or back screens is probably the most difficult part of platform tennis to learn and eventually master. But it is a vital and essential ingredient of the game, if you aspire to becoming a top player and competitor.

If you have played any squash or four-wall handball, you should be able to understand the angles and racquet work required for platform tennis far more readily than the individual who has played neither.

The best (and actually only) way to learn the "wire work" is practice, practice, and *more practice*. There is no substitute and no easy way. No book has been written that can tell you precisely where to stand to retrieve a ball off the wires. There are too many angles and too many variables.

If the screens are true and tight (and each court seems to vary somewhat) a ball angled into the screen will come off at the same angle. This is a fundamental law of geometry. Another variable, besides the tension of the wires, is, of course, the speed at which the ball is hit into the screen.

Back Screen: Most beginners have trouble with the ball coming off the back screen primarily for one reason: They normally wait until the ball is practically on top of them before making their backswing. They wind up and swing their paddle at the last possible instant.

There is a beautiful rhythm to screen play, and in order to feel relaxed and comfortable in returning the ball off the wire, it is most important that you take your backswing as the *ball goes* by *you,* and into the screen. In so doing your paddle is *behind* the ball and ready to make a smooth, effortless return as the ball rebounds out. This early backswing avoids a last-second "flick" (frequently a "whiff") or an uncontrolled return.

Another basic precept of all screen play is to position your feet and body whenever possible behind the ball prior to hitting. It is always better to go too far into the screen and then follow the ball out, rather than to be too far in front of it to be able to obtain the leverage or strength to smack the ball back. Don't wait for the ball to come out to you. Go in after it!

The vast majority of your returns off the back (as well as side) wires will be lobs. Your opponents are both up at net and you and your partner are in the back court on the defense.

Most beginners or mediocre players do not *use* the back screen enough. They somehow feel that it exists only as a last resort, a crutch, when all else has failed, or when their opponents have laced a ball by them. This is a completely erroneous concept, mainly brought on by fear of screen play through inexperience. They do not understand that it is very possible to play the ball off the back screen to an *advantage*. A lack of confidence frequently causes them to cut the ball off before it reaches the back screen. Again, a hurried, off-balance stroke can often cause errors and lost points. *Wait!* You really have a great deal of time, and the back screen can be a friendly and helpful ally.

Women especially have little or no concept as to how to play balls off the back wire. They rarely hit the ball hard or deep enough when they are playing each other to bring on many screen shots. When these women enter mixed doubles tournaments, and their male opponents slam an overhead past them, most of them are apt to scream, giggle, freeze (usually in that order) and automatically say "nice shot." Meanwhile the ball has rebounded off the back wire and could easily have been returned if she had had some concept of how to hit a screen shot.

Often you have seen both men and women make a hurried, frantic half-volley of a deep, hard shot at the base line and dump the ball into the net. If they had only stepped aside, allowed the ball to go into the back screen (which, in turn, allows them *more time!*) and taken it as it came back, their percentage of errors would be drastically reduced.

The superior female competitors nowadays often do not have better ground strokes or net games than many other women. You will notice, however, that most of the top gals are in their forties. It has taken them that many years to gain enough experience with screen play (gained from competing in mixed doubles tournaments) to be relaxed, and to be able to return their opposition's shots off the screen in a steady and effective manner. More than anything else, their knowledge of the screens sets them apart.

Let me quickly add a word, however, to all women players. You need *not* be forty before your screen play sets you apart from the rest of the women. If the particular foursome with whom you play doesn't hit the ball hard enough to require back screen play, you and your partner can practice alone. Have her stand on the other side of the court, up front toward the net. Being in the forecourt will make it easier for her to hit the ball deep and into the back screen. Keep lobbing to her so that she can hit overheads hard and high into the side and back wires for you to retrieve. You will be absolutely amazed how a fifteen-minute workout once or twice a week in this manner will improve your screen play and give you poise and confidence. In other words, girls, don't neglect (or be afraid of) screen play. It is an integral part of the game, especially if you aspire to compete with good competition in mixed doubles tournaments.

So, men *and* women, once you have become proficient and sure of your screen play, there is no reason why you cannot make an *offensive* shot off the back screen if your opponents hit a ball that comes out high and far enough.

With experience you will quickly learn when the "right shot" occurs; that is, a ball that rebounds off the wires and affords you the time, opening and opportunity to "ram it," low and hard, right at or in between your startled opponents.

If you see that your offensive shot off the screen has caught your adversaries off-balance, it pays to follow into the net behind the ball. Frequently the element of surprise, plus the effect of the shot, will cause your opponents to make a weak return and you can volley it away for a winner.

Side Screen: A ball that hits deep in your court first against the side and then the back screen is somewhat more difficult to return than one that goes directly into the back screen.

Practically all *forehand* court players will *back up* on a ball that travels from the side to the back wire, and return it off of his forehand.

Many players on the *backhand* side of the court do not necessarily back up and return off their backhand. Some of them turn with the ball, pivoting their bodies, following the ball around, and take it on their forehand. You can try both styles as you learn, and decide for yourself what approach is best for you.

Here again, it is a matter of playing and practicing in order to learn the angles, and how the speed of your opponent's shots will affect these angles. The *only* answer to feeling comfortable on side-back screen shots is to practice, and *keep practicing*. This is the one and only way to learn these angles, and where you should position yourself to make effortless (and even sometimes effective) returns.

A shot hit softly by the opposition had better be picked off as it rebounds off the side wire *before* it goes into the back wire, or it might well die before you can return it. A hard-hit shot will, on the other hand, rebound far out into the court, and you will have to hustle forward to be in the right spot to return it.

A ball going into the corner and rebounding parallel to the side wire (a "hugger") is best "scooped off" rather than "picked off." That is to say, run the edge of your paddle along the wire surface, with the playing area of the paddle at right angles to the screen. With a loose wrist try to "wipe" or "scrape" the clinging ball off the screen and over to your opponent's side of the net. Your chances of making a satisfactory return by employing this "safer" technique of scooping a side wire "hugger" are far better than trying to pick the ball off—which frequently results in an error.

On side-back screen shots, as with *all* platform tennis strokes,

Ted Winpenny, one of the finest "backhand" court players in the game, is seen falling into the side wire to return a high one off the screen on his forehand. He and the author were finalists in the Nationals (1965). and annexed the crown the following year with the loss of only 21 games in 15 sets of competition. Note how his paddle is up and back behind the ball.

it is most important to get your racquet back as quickly as you can. Even as you are going after the ball and following it as it rebounds off the screens, pull your racquet back and have it in a ready, cocked position prior to hitting. A last-minute windup will frequently result in a miss or an error.

As with straight in and out back wire shots, when the right opportunity presents itself along the side screen, there is absolutely no reason why you must continue to lob or feel as if you have to remain on the defensive. If one of your opponent's shots comes out far and high enough, you can certainly try to "pop it" hard and make an offensive return. Practice and experience will tell you when this opportunity arrives.

Another fundamental rule for ground strokes holds true for screen shots; that is, whenever possible, try to get *down* to the level of the ball. On many occasions when hitting the side-back wire returns you will be attempting to return a ball that is slowly dying (nearing the playing deck). You will have to "dig" for it. Your chances of success will be greatly enhanced if you *bend your knees* and hit from a crouched position.

SCREEN PLAY RECAP:

1. Screen play is the most *difficult* part of platform tennis to learn, and there is absolutely no substitute for *practice*.

2. Take your backswing as the *ball goes by you,* and into the screen. Your paddle must be *behind* the ball as it rebounds.

3. Position your feet and body behind the ball prior to hitting. Do not wait for the ball to come out to you—*go in after it!*

4. Use the screens to an *advantage. Wait!* You have far more time than you think.

5. An *offensive* shot can be returned off the screens once you master the rhythm, angles and timing and feel comfortable in returning wire shots.

6. *Women* can be just as adept as men if they will *practice* screen play.

7. *Scrape* off side screen "huggers" rather than try to pick off.

8. Bend your knees and "dig" for low, dying balls.

CHAPTER 7

The Volley

The forehand or backhand volley in platform tennis is hit the same way as in practically any other racquet game. The chief difference, again, is that the back screen precludes, for the most part, the opportunity to "spank" a hard-hit drive-volley past your opponents and away for a clean, outright winner. The back screen means that your adversaries always have a chance to retrieve anything, even when the ball has passed them and appears to be "ungettable."

Essentially the volley is hit with a slightly downward "jab" or block, with the wrist cocked and the paddle head up and slightly open. Tilt back your paddle face 15 to 20 degrees from the 90-degree (perpendicular) plane employed for ground strokes. The back spin will enable you to take some of the speed off the oncoming ball.

When you become accustomed to volleying with a slight underspin, you will more easily be able to pull off an effective drop volley (Chapter 9) from the same starting position. This shot can be a very potent weapon in platform tennis.

No wind-up or backswing is necessary when volleying. Of all the basic strokes, the paddle should be held as *tightly* as possible on the volley to make absolutely certain it doesn't budge or get pushed backwards upon impact with the ball. So squeeze your bat handle prior to meeting the ball when volleying. A slight bit of wrist action is employed on the volley, but in a regimented and firm manner.

In addition, try to reach out *in front* of you to meet the ball.

Gordon Gray and Jesse Sammis are at net. Picture shows Gray making a low backhand volley. Notice that his paddle is tilted back and open to help the ball clear the top of the net. His knees are bent and his weight is forward.

Jesse Sammis is hitting a forehand volley. The paddle face is slightly open, his wrist is cocked and firm, and the paddle head is up just prior to striking the ball. Gray, as always, is ready. His racquet is up, his eyes are riveted on the ball, and his weight is evenly distributed on the soles of his feet.

Whenever possible avoid allowing the ball to come in too close to your body.

Your *short,* abbreviated *follow-through* should be *out* and *down* in the direction of where you want the ball to go. The follow-through of your paddle head should be pointing right at the very top of the net. The volley is more of a *punch* than a stroke. Through practice and more practice, you will eventually learn how hard and how deep, or how short and how softly, you can and should hit the ball in order to place it in a difficult or strategic spot in your opponents' court.

Remember you need not always go for a winner in the back corners. An occasional volley straight down the *middle* of your opponents' court, one that does not come out too far, can also be an effective shot, especially when you are playing against a right-handed and a left-handed team. In that case your opponents will usually have two backhands down the middle. Unless a team has played together for a long time, there is frequently a moment of hesitation and indecision as to who will take shots down the middle.

The inexperienced player will usually have less of a problem hitting a forehand volley properly, but can and usually does run into difficulties on the backhand side. When attempting to apply backspin to backhand volleys utilizing the necessary downward slicing motion, he often makes the mistake of raising the elbow upward. Raising the elbow certainly helps put backspin on the ball, but it also causes one to hit *too far* on the underside of the ball. The result is frequently a ball popped straight up rather than the crisp, low "skidder" intended.

When hitting a backhand volley, *keep your elbow down;* it will help you to hit the ball on the backside rather than the underside. Two exercises are recommended for overcoming this common problem and each is practiced best when someone merely throws a ball right at your paddle while you are at net. In this way you need not be concerned with form, and can concentrate on the position of your elbow:

In one drill use your left hand to keep your hitting elbow down and next to the body. In the other, press a ball against your body, using your right elbow, while hitting. Either procedure will enable you to acquire the feel of the proper elbow position in making a backhand volley.

Preferably (and again, there frequently isn't enough time) try to get your body out of the way by turning *sideways* to the net prior to hitting your volley. In addition, try to lunge forward, your body weight moving into the ball. Do not back up as you are volleying. Leaning back on your heels will cause inconsistent and erratic shots on *all* of your strokes.

When at net while your partner is serving, your paddle head should be up (slightly higher than the top of the net) and out in front of you. Cradle the paddle loosely in your left hand, and from this position you are ready to move in any direction with one motion. Your feet should be comfortably apart, with your weight forward on your toes. Flex your knees, and bend over slightly from the waist. The proper position is approximately 3 to 4 feet from the net. This is the "ready position." By having your racquet up and forward, you are prepared to volley practically any ball you can reach with the minimum amount of effort.

While at net it is perfectly good sportsmanship to feign "poaching" or to move across the court, parallel to the net, after your partner has served. Such movements will concern and worry your opponents. They might think you are going across to cut off, or volley, their cross court return of service. They may, therefore, conceivably hit too wide on the cross court return in an effort to hit the ball out of reach of the poacher.

Or they might attempt to "keep you honest" and aim the return down your alley. If you were only faking the poach you will already be in the proper position to make an easy volley, and allow your partner that much more time to take an offensive position at the net.

Finally, by being active and animated at net, you will be breaking your opponents' concentration and confidence in their returns of service. They will begin to try to "outguess" you, to anticipate whether or not you are going to move across, and they should really be putting their efforts solely into hitting the ball back. You will help win many serves for your partner by employing this moving-about tactic.

Gordon Gray assumes the proper "ready position" at net while his partner, Sammis, serves. (Note his form.) Gray's knees are slightly flexed, the paddle is up and in the center of his body, and he is bent over at the waist. He is, indeed, ready to move or hit in any direction necessary. Note the concentration reflected in Gray's face.

The team that controls the net position the majority of the time will invariably win. Above, in the foreground are Peter and Wendy Chase, a husband-wife combination who have won many matches in National Mixed Doubles competition. Wendy was 1976 National Women's Champion teamed with Linda Wolf.

VOLLEY RECAP:

1. Platform tennis volleys are similar to tennis volleys. Essentially they are downward *"jabs"* with the *paddle head up* and slightly *open*.

2. *Hold* paddle *tightly, no wind-up* is necessary, and reach *out* in *front* to volley. Practically *no backswing* is necessary.

3. Keep your elbow *down*.

4. Volley *deep* and *not too hard*. Aim *frequently* for the *corners* and *occasionally* down the middle.

5. *Bend your knees* and *open* the paddle (tilt back) on *low* returns.

6. When your partner is serving "poach" occasionally or feign poaching to keep the opponents honest and edgy.

CHAPTER 8

The Return-of-
Service Volley

Unlike lawn tennis, the platform tennis player does *not* have the option of going or not going in to net behind his service. He (and she, for that matter) *must* follow in behind the serve. There is no such formation in platform tennis as one partner up at net and one partner back. Either you are both up or both back if you are to be effective, the one exception being "blitzing."

It is important to move in as *far* as you can behind your service before making that first volley. The ideal court position for volleying your opponents' return of serve is *inside* (toward the net) your own service line. If you come in fast enough, and your service is effective enough, you should be able to advance at least to this desired position. It means, of course, that you cannot make your approach casual. You really have to *charge* the net in order to be in the proper position to make that first critical volley.

Come to net, therefore, as far as you can, but you should try to become "anchored," with the feet planted firmly on the deck, at the moment you make that first volley. If you are still moving forward at the time the ball strikes your paddle, the chances are good that the ball will sail out of court because of the momentum of your forward movement.

The return-of-service volley is one of the most difficult shots in the game of platform tennis. Why? Because, unless you have executed a near perfect service, the return of serve, as mentioned earlier, is one of the few strokes that your opponent can really wind up for and "powder." If your service "hangs fat," as they say, either you or your poor defenseless partner at net might very well end up "eating" the ball—or at least be called upon to make a weak, defensive "pushy" volley.

The correct spot for you to aim that first volley is *deep* into your opponents' back court, preferably toward the *rear corners* to keep them both back and away from the net. It is practically impossible to hit a clean winner off a return-of-service volley, even when your opponents' return is high and ineffective. Remember, both your opponents are in the back court. The main purpose of this first volley, therefore, is to provide the opportunity and the time for you to assume the proper net position. This position is approximately the same distance away from the net as your partner, both of you forming an offensive, protective, and impenetrable wall. Remember the number one rule of winning platform tennis is: "The team that has control of the net the majority of the time will invariably win."

RETURN-OF-SERVICE VOLLEY RECAP:

1. Move in as *close* to the *net* as you possibly can behind your serve in order to volley the return.

2. Be *anchored* at the moment you make the volley.

3. Volley *deep* in your opponents' court—preferably toward the *rear corners*.

4. *Rarely* go for a *winner*—essentially hit the return-of-service volley for better positioning at net.

CHAPTER 9

The Drop Volley

Only a few of the top-ranking platform tennis players today employ the drop volley effectively. For those who lack a real "touch" or "feel" of the ball on the paddle head, it is an extremely difficult shot to hit with any degree of consistency. And, if you do not hit it perfectly, you will end up in serious trouble. You and your partner will be at net with your opponents charging in to make an easy putaway, because your drop volley "dropped" too high or too deep in your opponents' court, and there you are standing at net an easy target for a lost point.

A drop volley is hit the same as a regular net shot, except that you should make every effort to "hold" your shot (hide your intentions) as long as possible. The stroke itself is actually performed with a very *short, deft* touch of the racquet to the ball.

Your chances of success are greatly enhanced if you are practically on *top* of the net rather than back in the usual volleying position (approximately 3 to 4 feet from the net).

The idea in hitting a drop volley is merely to touch the ball with a short, chopping, undercut motion, allowing it barely to clear the net, drop straight down and die. The well-executed drop volley will bounce on the other side no farther than 3 or 4 inches from the net. Even if your opponents have anticipated your shot and can get up to the ball, retrieval is almost impossible because of the ball's proximity to the net.

The follow-through is not quite the same on the drop volley as with the regular volley. When the ball makes contact with your paddle you just barely *touch* it, then quickly withdraw the paddle (rather than following through in the direction of the net). The drop volley is the ultimate in "touch."

Depending upon where your opponents are, either a straight drop (right in front of you) or a sharply angled, cross court drop volley aimed at the side screen can be equally effective.

Remember also, as with all your volleying shots, after execution be sure to plant your feet and have your paddle up and out in front of you in anticipation of possible retrieval by your opponents. Do not take any shot for granted!

DROP VOLLEY RECAP:

1.   The drop volley is probably the most *difficult* shot to hit effectively and consistently.

2.   You must be practically *on top of the net*.

3.   *Barely touch* the ball and aim to *just clear the net*. Attempt to *apply backspin* with an open paddle.

4.   *Be prepared* for your opponents to retrieve the ball.

CHAPTER 10

The Half Volley

This is another basic stroke which really cannot be taught. Possessing fast reflexes is, indeed, helpful, but there are some fundamentals to keep in mind that can help your half volleying.

A half volley is essentially a defensive shot. The opposition has hit the ball right at your feet, and you have been caught in the embarrassing position (usually *out of position*) where you can neither volley nor get back in time to hit a ground stroke. The half volley is usually hit when you have been caught somewhere around the service line.

Since you are in trouble you should immediately forget about everything except *keeping your eye on the ball!* This will help you to coordinate your paddle so that at least you will have a chance to block the shot back.

Another important precept when half volleying is to get your paddle *back* and *down* low enough to catch the ball just as it starts to rise off the playing deck. This means that you should have your knees flexed and that your entire body, from the waist up, should be bent.

You will hardly have any time to take a backswing. Hit through smoothly, but with far less follow-through than employed with your *offensive volley*. Keep the paddle face *open* in order to allow the ball a fair chance of clearing the net. All the rest is "a little bit of luck," timing, and, again, just playing and practicing.

Scotty Pierce, a hard-hitting left-hander, is shown bending his knees for either a volley or a reflex half volley. See how he gets down to the level of the ball and reaches out in front to make the volley. His arm is stiff and his wrist firm. Note, also, his eyes glued on the ball.

HALF VOLLEY RECAP:

1. *Watch* the ball *closely.*

2. Catch low balls *on the rise, bend your knees,* and have your paddle open.

3. The half volley is primarily a *defensive* shot hit, by necessity, when you are out of position.

CHAPTER 11

The Lob

The lob is a frequently employed stroke in the game of platform tennis. The key to hitting a *good* lob is to try to obtain as much *depth* as you can. Whether you hit your lob from a shot rebounding off the platform deck or the screens try, whenever possible, to lob deep. Height is important, but secondary to length.

Generally speaking, there are four occasions when you must or should lob:

1. For defensive reasons, when you are in serious trouble and have no recourse but to lob to stay in the point.
2. As an unexpected change of pace.
3. When your opponents are hovering too close to the net.
4. For tactical reasons. For example, your opponents do not know how to put a lob away, or the sun might be directly in their eyes, etc.

The majority of lobs are hit as defensive shots; that is, when your opposition is at the net and has placed a ball that forces you out of position. As you can see from the different occasions when you should lob, there are actually two different *types* of lobs—the defensive one and the offensive one.

The perfect *offensive* lob is hit rather low, so that the arc of the flight of the ball *just clears* your opponent's outstretched paddle. Needless to say, this shot takes a great deal of practice, but it is an integral part of your repertoire of strokes.

To be an effective lobber, it is most important to get your paddle back as quickly as possible. In other words, be prepared well

Gloria Dillenbeck, several times Women's Doubles champion, is seen lofting a lob from deep in the backhand or ad side of the court. Her eyes are right on the ball, the paddle face is open and her body weight is on the forward foot. She is properly hitting the ball both up and out in order to make an effective high and deep lob.

In the background is an attractive warming hut. Such a building is an integral part of any platform tennis set-up. It is the center of conviviality and après-paddle camaraderie. Large picture windows provide the watchers with an unobstructed view of the action on the court.

in advance, which will help you disguise your shot. In addition, and to realize the greatest results, it is best to "hold" your shot and hide your intentions until the very last minute. By so doing, your opponents will tend to be leaning forward in anticipation of a hard return, which will aid your efforts to drop the ball over their heads and beyond their reach. If hit correctly there is very little chance of retrieval off the back screen. Most lobs are expected (when you are in trouble), but the unexpected lob can be an offensive "gem." The element of surprise—when your opponent is anticipating a hard-hit, low, passing shot and you lob—is a great offensive tactic. So get your paddle back quickly and your feet in the proper position as though ready to drill a hard passing shot; a lob at this moment will be a most effective stroke.

Needless to say, if your lob successfully clears your opponents' paddles and they are forced to relinquish the net, be sure you and your partner take advantage of your good shot to *gain* the net. Their normal return, if your ball does not die on the back wire, will probably also be a lob.

Keep in mind that the lob is a full stroke and not a short, quick stroke. You must follow through. The backswing is the same as for your ground strokes, which, again, will help you to disguise your lob. A quarterback in football employs the same windup for a short, "over the middle" pass as he does for a 60-yard "bomb" —only the follow-through varies. In platform tennis the follow-through, when hitting a lob, is somewhat more elevated than on a ground stroke, but don't think of hitting the ball only *up,* concentrate on hitting it *out and up*.

Attempt to place your lob toward the *backhand* side of your opponents. This will cause them to hit their overheads from an off-balance, awkward position, and oftentimes will result in a poorly hit ball or an error.

Finally, a high lob down the *center* frequently brings on confusion between the opponents, especially if they have not played together as a team for too long. Each one will think the other is going to take it.

LOB RECAP:

1. One of the most *frequently* employed strokes in the game of platform tennis.

2. Two different types of lobs: *defensive* and *offensive*.

3. On offensive lobs, *"hold"* your shot as long as you can.

4. Get your paddle back *quickly,* as suggested for all platform tennis strokes.

5. Follow through *upwards,* as well as *outwards.*

6. Aim your lobs toward the *backhand* side of your opposition.

7. Lob down the *center* to bring on possible confusion.

8. *Depth* rather than *height* is the key to an effective lob.

CHAPTER 12

The Overhead

Basically the overhead is hit with the same motion as its counterpart in lawn tennis. When your opponents lob and they will *often,* especially if you and your partner have been soundly trouncing them), as you go back to the ball (and start back as quickly as possible in order to be in a position prior to hitting), bring your racquet back to the initial phase of the overhead smash. Do not wait until the ball starts dropping toward you to bring your paddle back behind your head in the cocked position. This wind-up is shorter than the more sweeping first stage of the service. The primary reason for the more abbreviated wind-up is that the lob is descending from a certain height and hitting it squarely and properly calls for exact timing. Ideally you should attempt to hit the ball on your overhead when it is located slightly to your right and a little in front of you.

Whenever possible, *jump up toward* the descending ball and have both feet off the deck at the moment of contact. This stretching or added height will aid you in driving the ball downward more sharply so that it bounces high in your opponents' court, and (you hope) either dies in one of the back corners, or kicks out so unexpectedly as to be irretrievable.

In addition, your arm should be extended to the limit at the moment the racquet meets the ball. If you are hitting with a bent elbow, you are letting your opponents' lob come down too far. The fully extended arm will also help you obtain those precious inches of additional height. Try to keep the ball in front of you

David Jennings, National Men's Doubles champion in 1964 and 1967 when paired with Oliver "Kim" Kimberly, shows excellent style in hitting a jump overhead. By leaving the deck and going up for the ball Dave has added many valuable inches to his height. Note his famous derby.

and not behind, where hitting a proper shot will not only feel awkward, but is next to impossible to make.

As with all platform tennis strokes, footwork is of vital importance when hitting an overhead. Your weight should be evenly distributed on the *balls* of your feet. Whenever possible it is desirable to jump for the overhead, and this, obviously, calls for precise timing. It is not easy to hit a jump overhead, and this is probably why so many players hit the ball with their feet planted firmly and flatly (and wrongly) on the platform deck. It is, however, extremely important to go up for the ball when you can. Never wait for your opponents' lob to come down too far, as it may come too close to your body and force you to hit from a cramped, bent-arm, awkward position. Your body will be hunched, rather than properly stretched out, and it will be difficult for you to hit through with a smooth, flowing, non-tiring stroke.

The vast majority of overheads are hit gently and deftly, and should be carefully aimed at the opposition's *back corners*. There is *no* reason to "smash" an overhead in platform tennis. In tennis, a powerfully hit overhead smash is usually "away" for a winner or over your opponent's head. In this game, however, a hard hit overhead will only rebound off the back screen and travel half way back to your side of the court. Unless it is wholly unexpected your opponents will then have an easy chance at a kill. (That back screen is, as mentioned before, a great equalizer).

The reason you should aim at your opponents' corners is that an almost sure winner occurs if your ball lands straight into the corner where the back and side wires meet. Frequently the ball will rebound in an unpredictable manner that makes retrieval practically impossible. That is to say, it will rebound either straight out and parallel to the side wire, or it will shoot out unexpectedly toward the middle of the court. Your competition will be startled, and only a miraculous reflex shot will give them any chance at all for recovery.

Occasionally a very hard-hit overhead *is* in order (say four or five times during the course of an average match) but only to keep your opponents "edgy."

Tommy Holmes has jumped for his overhead and displays perfect form in executing the stroke. See how his elbow is straight
and he is hitting down on the ball. Tommy is one of only a few
players who wears a glove on his "hitting" hand. In 1965 he and his
partner, Mike O'Hearn, annexed the National Doubles crown.

Change of pace in any racquet game is most important. Doing the unexpected, the unpredictable, will prevent your opponents from anticipating where the ball will go. If *all* your overheads are aimed to bounce in the corner and to die back there, your opponents will tend to hang deep in their back court. A *hard* smashed overhead will frequently find your opponents off guard and not able to catch up to the ball as it rebounds far out in the court.

For the same reason it is well to hit a few overheads straight down the *middle* to draw them away from protecting their corners, and perhaps cause confusion as to who is to take the shot off the back screen.

Since there is no premium on power, the most important aspect of your platform tennis overhead is that it be *consistent*. Certainly placement is also a significant factor, but secondary compared to your displaying steadiness and confidence when hitting the shot.

In doubles it is sometimes difficult to decide whether you or your partner should hit the overhead that is aimed down the middle. Generally, the player in the right hand (backhand) side of the court should take it. He has a better view of a ball coming down the center of the court. He also can more quickly discern what the opponents are doing and where they are. The backhand court partner will not be backing away or moving to his left; but going to his right to hit the overhead, which is less awkward and far easier for right-handed players.

A "call system," where either you or your partner calls "mine," is very important with any team. This call should be *respected* between partners, even though one might very well have to travel somewhat farther than his partner.

Finally, if one player on a team has a better, more consistent overhead, he should hit the majority of the shots, provided he is in a reasonably good position to take them.

OVERHEAD RECAP:

1. *Power* means very little. *Placement, deftness,* and *steadiness* are of paramount importance.

2. *Jump up* toward the descending ball, and meet it with a *fully extended* hitting arm out in *front*.

3. Aim for the opponents' *back corners*.

4. The partner on the *backhand* side should usually hit overheads when opponents' lobs are down the *middle*.

5. *Call* to determine who hits the overhead.

CHAPTER 13

Basic Doubles Tactics

The last platform tennis singles tournament was played over forty years ago. The sport does not lend itself to any kind of fun at singles because the man at net has an overwhelming advantage over his opponent.

All kinds of handicap ideas have been suggested and tried (*e.g.*, the server cannot come in behind his serve until his opponent has returned his ball and it bounces once, etc.), but the appeal is just not there.

Since it is impractical to play singles competitively (although you can certainly practice your strokes with your partner), you should attempt to learn as much of the basic strategy and tactics of platform tennis doubles as you can.

Select Your Partner: When picking your partner, first and foremost try to find one who is at least as good as you are—preferably *better*. In addition, you should have a personality rapport with him. If you are both shy or defensive players or, on the other hand, all-out hitters, you will not make a good team. Your partner should complement you. A team consisting of two players who want to be "captain" or the star will never make a great team.

The most effective winning teams are usually composed of a daring hard-hitter and a "steady Eddie" conservative type, an extrovert who parties it up all Saturday night while his partner is in bed by 9:00, a gambler and a miser. Compatible blending of diverse personalities is just as important as putting a good forehand player with a powerful backhand player, or an excellent volleyer with a fine server.

Partners *must* get along as people, especially in a game that is played in such a confined area and has so many frustrating and tense moments. So, if you are the dominant type of individual, look for a fellow who is a follower. If you are the kind that has to be led, look for a leader. No matter what, select a partner in whom you have confidence. "It takes two to tango," and there never has been a truly great doubles combination where the superior player covered 80% of the court. It is impractical and physically impossible.

In platform tennis doubles you will discover, for some reason or other, that you are able to play either the forehand or backhand court much better than the other side. You will rarely hear anyone say, "Smith is a tremendous, all-around performer." He is either a "tremendous forehand" or a "fine backhand" court player.

Usually with the better players the one with the stronger backhand will be more comfortable covering the forehand court, and the person with a superior forehand will play the backhand side more adroitly. This is because in top-flight competition the majority of serves are hit down the *middle* in order to reduce the angle of the return. The person playing the forehand court, therefore, will be compelled to return many serves off his backhand, and it is essential that he have confidence in his backhand. The individual on the backhand court, however, can more readily "run around" any serves aimed at his backhand and drill a hard forehand return.

In addition, both players have their strongest ground stroke shot when the ball is hit down the middle.

Notice the top teams in competition. Whenever they are forced to "cover" for each other by retrieving the opponents' shots in the opposite back corners, at the first opportunity they will cross back to their more familiar side. It can be pathetic to watch a fine right court player pinned in the left court corner, looking as awkward as a roller skater on ice.

For beginners, however, the general rule of thumb should be that the better player should play the backhand or left court. This side demands slightly more skill, and the opponents almost subconsciously will play the majority of their shots to the backhand side. Also, more "key" points will be served to the "ad" court. The novice will quickly decide that he somehow feels more at home on one side or the other, and that is where he should play. Then he ought to "specialize" and become as skillful as possible on that side, and not attempt to master both sides equally.

There is some indefinable quality that the better teams seem to develop between players, and, for a lack of a better word, I call it "chemism." It is a "feeling" of knowing exactly where your partner is even if you cannot see him.

It is also a "sensing" of what shots are yours and what are his. It is knowing precisely where he will hit his shot at any given moment. This chemism is developed, and doesn't just happen. It takes years of experience under rigorous and trying competitive play.

So, "once you have found him, never let him go." Stay together and play in as many tournaments as possible. You might not find the all-important chemism with another player who seemingly is better. Remember, in order to be a successful team, it takes *two!*

Suggestions for Improving Doubles Play:

1.   When your partner is receiving service (unlike tennis), you should be back at the baseline with him. Going part of the way in, as the better tennis players do, is dangerous, and involves committing yourself needlessly. Unless your partner hits a perfect, low return, you will be caught in a most precarious and often embarrassing position. In addition, moving in can be distracting to your partner since he will spot you out of the corner of his eye.

If, on the other hand, you see that your partner has hit a fine return that will force your opponents to hit up, or to make a feeble, defensive volley, there is no reason at all why you can't charge the net and cut off their return and volley it for a winner. Remember, except when you "blitz" behind your return of service and charge in, the rule of thumb for platform tennis strategy is that a team moves up and back *together!*

2.   The partner who is winning his service more easily and reg-

ularly should always start serving first in each set. This is allowed by the rules and just makes good sense. Perhaps the only exception is when a lefty and a righty are paired together. There is no point in having both of you serving with the sun in your eyes when both of you can serve with the sun at your backs.

3. Whenever either you or your partner has an option or doubt as to where to hit the ball, drill your ground strokes down the middle. The old "center theory" has been employed successfully in lawn tennis for many years, and by many great doubles teams. This tried and true tactic works even better in platform tennis because of the closeness of the opposition, not only to you, but to each other. The chances of confusion, hesitation and uncertainty are great.

4. When your opponents hammer the middle, who should cover the shot? After you have played with a partner for a period of time an understanding will eventually develop as to which of you protects the center area. There are three rules to follow, however, that work quite well:

a) The player who is *closest to the net* should cover a shot down the middle; the idea being that he has a better chance of "cutting off" the ball sooner.

b) Or the player who last hit the ball should logically be more ready to cover the return down the middle.

c) Or the partner on the *backhand* side should protect the center when both members of the team are equidistant from the net. The theory here is that the backhand court player (assuming he is right-handed) can volley better utilizing his forehand.

On lobs over the middle, the same principle holds true. The partner on the backhand side will have a better shot from a less awkward position than the player on the forehand.

5. Most of the superior teams playing competitively have worked out a system of *calling* for shots—some more constantly and vociferously than others. Calling out "mine" or "yours" is an excellent idea, especially since the court is so small and the playing area more confined than in other racquet sports.

You must establish an understanding with your partner that

A shot hit down the opponents' center of the court can frequently cause confusion. Kim Kimberly and David Jennings, two-time National champions, confirm this fact in the above photograph.

if one of you calls for a shot, his judgment be held inviolate. Even if you believe you have a better shot at the ball than he has, respect his call and stay away.

6. The more skilled players have developed a valuable asset known as "having a good eye." This is the ability to predict prac-

tically the instant a ball leaves the opponent's paddle that it is going out of the court's playing area. A "good eye" can tell when a shot is going to be out if only by a few inches.

This ability too is usually obtained only after years of play. Many beginners face the problem of continually hitting "out" balls. They just cannot resist the temptation and find it extremely difficult to get their paddles out of the way in time. And how many costly points have been lost that way! If they had only dropped their paddles the point would have been theirs. It takes as much practice, as much good judgment, and just as fast reflexes to pull your racquet away as it does to get it up in order to make a fine volley.

Here again, a *calling system* will help immeasurably. If you feel the shot is definitely going out, say (loudly) "Out!" The sound of your voice will actually *help* your partner to remove his paddle out of the path of the ball—it's a signal that seems to *trigger* his reflexes. It is truly amazing how this works.

Obviously, as with calling "mine" or "yours," you must develop a faith in your partner's eye, and he in yours. When you reach that stage it will be worth at least one point a game to you, since most players hit that many out balls in a match. Letting an out ball go is tantamount to a walk in baseball. What easier way to get on first base, or win a point?

7.   Generally speaking, you should lob frequently, drop volley rarely, and drop shot never. When you have a sure putaway (if there is any such thing in platform tennis), put it away. Don't hit the hard shot; go for the obvious, certain winner.

8.   Vary your return of service and disguise it as much as you can. *Hold* all your shots as long as you can. This will help prevent the opponents from anticipating where you plan to hit the ball. *Change of pace* and *steadiness* are the keys to winning platform tennis, not overwhelming power.

9.   When your partner is serving and you are at the net, poach occasionally. You will be able to hit a few winning volleys. Your opponents will be extra-careful on their returns, and you will be helping your partner to win his service. Remember a person's

service is apt to be only as effective as his net man is. In this game, of all racquet sports, it takes *two* to win. A "singles star" will be a lonely loser!

10. Do not, whatever you do, ever glare at your partner or moan when he misses an easy shot, or fails to get that big point for you. He is doing his very best and really wants to win as badly as you do. Pat him on the back and tell him to "forget it," and mean it. There will be other big points and important matches. Show him that you have complete faith in him and his ability. To play winning platform tennis you must have confidence in your own game, as well as in your partner's. It behooves you not to shake your partner's concentration or display any frustration.

11. Don't allow "close calls" against you, or "let cords" that drop over on your side of the court, discourage you. It truly is amazing how these adverse breaks tend to even out over the course of a match.

12. When you and your partner have pulled one of your opponents wide over to the backhand court and you are both at net, your concern should be to cover your forehand alley and the center, leaving your backhand alley relatively open. The reverse holds true on a wide ball to your opponents' forehand court. By so doing, you will be "cutting off" the angle of your opposition's probable return. It is very unlikely that they can hit such a wide cross court angle for a winner from such an off the court position. In other words "float" in the direction of the ball.

13. Never change a winning style, and always change a losing one. There is an old proverb that says: "Never change horses in the middle of the stream." That statement might be amended with ". . . unless the horse is losing ground to the current."

If you are being severely thrashed by a team you feel you should beat, have a little conference with your partner as you change sides on the odd game. Discuss between yourselves what you have been doing wrong, and decide how you plan to change your tactics.

Perhaps you are not being aggressive enough, or perhaps the circumstances call for steadiness. You might be playing the

John Beck, who has won U.S. titles in both Men's (with Herb FitzGibbon) and Mixed Doubles (with his sister, Sue Wasch), is pictured hitting a low forehand return. John is six feet five, and therefore has to do a great deal of knee-bending in order to get down to the level of the ball on his ground strokes.

stronger of your two opponents, or even worse you are not hammering away at their weaknesses.

It is just not enough to say, "Come on, let's get hot." It is not always that easy to pull your games together and to "get up." The mark of a good doubles team is one that can find and exploit the opponents' weaknesses and eventually win the match even when they are having an off day.

14.   When a southpaw and a righthanded player are paired up it is usually best for the lefty to play the right side of the court. This statement assumes the two players are about equal in ability. It is, generally, easier for most players to return shots rebounding from the side and/or back screens off the forehand. This capability more than offsets the possible problems encountered when covering shots down the middle with two backhands.

15.   Faithfully employ and practice the fundamental strokes set forth in this book. Don't regress to that old grip or old stroke you have been using for years just because you and your partner find yourselves behind. The principles promulgated in the earlier chapters are sound and will improve your game as long as you practice them—both in "fun" matches as well as under the pressure of competition.

16.   The best advice I can offer to a beginner is to *study the styles* of the top players in the game today. This book gives you sound instructions relative to the basic fundamentals and strategy of platform tennis, but everyone still has his own unique and individualized style that seems to work for him.

CHAPTER 14

Competitive Mixed Doubles

No book on platform tennis could possibly be considered complete without a chapter on the subject of mixed doubles (troubles?)

Platform tennis is the only bat and ball sport in which the female partner has an excellent opportunity to hold her own. If she is proficient off the screens, is content to allow her partner to cover as much of the court as he possibly can, and concentrates primarily on being steady when protecting her own territory, she is well along the way to becoming a most desirable mixed doubles player.

In *most cases* (certainly not all the time) the woman is the weaker member of the team. She must, therefore, realize that she will be tormented, hit at, and played unmercifully by her opponents. She must be prepared to accept this punishment as being part of the game.

There is nothing more disconcerting than being unable to wear down the distaff members of the opposing team. Undramatic *steadiness* rather than occasional sensational shot-making usually is the woman's lot in a mixed doubles match.

Most of the better women players today are a level above the others not because of their power or their ability to hit devastating, clean winners. They are effective because of their willingness to display restraint, patience, and tenacity. So if the woman is the weaker member of the team, she should let her male partner be the aggressive and exciting shot-maker. She allows him to win the majority of points, to hit the majority of shots, and to cover the majority of the court.

In addition to this very basic understanding, there are other key strategies and tactics to be employed. And for all of them we have assumed that the man is the stronger player:

1. The male should play the *backhand* side of the court. It is a more difficult side from which to return service, the screen play is harder to master, and more important "key points" are made or saved from the right or "ad" court. It is also easier for the male to hit the opponents' lobs from the backhand court, and he will be able to cover shots down the middle with his forehand ground strokes and/or volley.

2. The man should always start serving. In this game you should ignore the ancient tradition of chivalry. Emily Post obviously never played platform tennis mixed doubles in competition when she advocated "ladies first"! The man should serve first even if it means his partner will have to serve with the sun in her eyes.

By being the first to serve, the odds are that he will have the opportunity of serving *more times* than his partner.

3. When the woman is serving, the man should "poach" (cross over toward the middle and attempt to pick off the return of service) *often*—far more frequently than would be considered prudent in men's doubles.

This tactic will harass and disconcert the opponents and will help the distaff partner to hold her service. It will, of course, work better when the woman is serving to her counterpart rather than to the opposing gentleman.

4. As a rule of thumb the man should be prepared to take *all* shots hit down the middle (it will also be his forehand). There should never be any doubt or hesitation (or quibbling) as to who should hit a particular ball. The answer is an unequivocal "the *man*"!

5. A very effective shot for a man to hit, especially early in the match, is a hard return of service right at the opposing female at net. Even if the woman ducks and the ball goes soaring out of the court, he has accomplished a great deal. This is tantamount to a pitcher "dusting back" a batter. She will very quickly realize

the man is playing to win, that beneath his gallant veneer there lies a burning desire to be victorious at any cost, and the "edginess" instilled in her will remain. Needless to say it will be worth many points to the man during the course of the match.

Obviously this shot should not be hit with the intent of physically harming the female. On the other hand, it is well to remember that there is no one more manageable than a player who has been caught off-balance and on the defensive.

6. As mentioned earlier the greatest asset the woman can offer her male partner is *steadiness*. This does *not* mean she should lob every shot back or "poop ball" every return. It merely suggests that she should make every effort to reduce her *errors* to an absolute minimum. Many more matches are lost because of costly errors than are won because of occasional crowd-pleasing winners. This is especially true in platform tennis, where a clean winner is far more difficult to make than in most racquet games. It has been calculated that 70% to 80% of all points scored are made on errors, not winners. Steadiness and consistency are the two most important words to remember.

7. A warning is in order also for the men. It is well to keep in mind that the male partner will see very few balls coming in his direction. He will have to stand by helplessly and watch his partner doggedly return one shot after another. He may edge slowly toward her side of the court hoping one of the opponents' balls will be placed near enough to him to get his paddle on it. What happens?

a) Usually he is not in the proper position and he makes a weak return, or

b) He has left his side of the court completely unguarded and the opponents volley a clean winner away in his unprotected corner, or

c) He will have the natural tendency to overcompensate— to try to do too much with the shot, and hence, an error results.

So, the man must also be patient. He must not try to do too much with the few balls that come in his direction. He should have the utmost confidence in his female partner's ability to with-

Charlotte Lee has won 14 National championships since 1961. With several different partners, she has annexed titles in both Women's and Mixed Doubles.

stand the barrage. He should be buttressed with the thought that on the next point they might well have the opposing female antagonist pinned in the corner. It is all part of the wonderful, fun-and-frustrating game of mixed doubles.

8. A very effective tactic for the man to employ when the female opponent serves is to "blitz," or go to net behind his return. Nothing will undermine the woman's confidence, or frustrate her partner at net more, than banging a low, hard return of service right at the woman coming to net. And, remember she *must* come to net behind her service. Innumerable faults will undoubtedly occur because she will be trying to hit her service a little deeper or a little harder than would be necessary if she did not have the pressure of a "blitzer" to contend with.

9. Lobbing a return of service directly over the female's head can do wonders to the opposing man's confidence in his ability to serve well and still cover the court. Unlike in tennis, it is practically impossible to kill a lob with an overhead smash. If you lob purposefully, the man who has just served and is coming to net will have to cross over behind his partner and make a high, weak defensive volley.

10. Finally, keep in mind that mixed doubles is a frustrating game that demands the utmost patience and a willingness by both partners to "hang on" and "ride out" the many moments of anguish. Be prepared for the lost opportunities and the frustrations and you will be a far better and happier mixed doubles player.

These points of strategy are to be employed when playing *competitive* platform tennis mixed doubles. You can be much more frivolous when playing your usual Saturday morning mixed doubles game at the local club against neighbors.

MIXED DOUBLES RECAP:

1. The woman, if she is the weaker player, should be *steady* and *errorless*.

2. The man should play the backhand side of the court and should *always* serve first.

3. The man should attempt to cut off as many shots as he can

while his partner is serving. He should also cover *all* shots down the middle.

4.   An early-in-the-match ploy is to drive a shot right at the female opponent. The purpose of this shot is to rattle but not hurt her.

5.   The man should frequently "blitz" when returning the opposing woman's serve. When the opposing woman's partner is serving, a lob over the woman's head at net is a winning tactic.

CHAPTER 15

Playing the Game

1. *Anticipation:* By definition, anticipating is the expectation or realization of an event in advance. In platform tennis, anticipation puts a player in the right place at the right time. While God-given reflexes and fast reactions are probably inborn, anticipation is not; it has to be acquired through competitive play, practice and experience.

One of the keys to anticipating where your opponent's ball is coming next is training your eyes to "pick up" the ball as it leaves his paddle. Take immediate note of the angle of the paddle face as well as the speed of the ball. An "instant study" of *the position of your opponent's feet* will also provide you with information as to where he plans to hit the ball. All of these data should register and, depending upon your natural reflexes and reactions, signal to you where you should move.

Experience will help you decide exactly what to do in a particular situation, and this experience is called "court know-how." Court know-how is the "sense" or instinctive knowledge that impels you to move in one direction or another. This "sense," unfortunately, cannot be taught. It has to be acquired through hard work and competition. When you have learned to correctly interpret the signals sent out by your opponent, you can anticipate what will probably be the "percentage" shot he will hit next, and will move in an instant to cover his shot.

How many times have you seen a better player who *frequently* is able to "plug up" a hole and make a miraculous recovery shot, or even volley or stroke his opponents' easy putaway for a winner? The first few times he does this, you accuse him of being "lucky"; but after a while, you realize he possesses this ability, and it sets him apart from the less experienced players.

Don't feel envious. You too, in time, can learn to anticipate, *if* you make sure to look for those signals when your opponent moves in to return your ball.

2. *Don't Let Up!:* One of the gravest mistakes a team can make is to "coast" or let up after gaining a lead over the opponents. Platform tennis, perhaps even more than any other racquet game, is a sport of *momentum.* Many a match has been won which seemed hopelessly lost. Letting up can destroy your concentration, and an apparently beaten team can gain confidence when the pressure is taken off. A few "sneaked" games, a few "let cords," and an avalanche of points and games against you can be the unhappy result.

Play every point as though it were an individual match—as if you were down match point and had to win it. This attitude, or strategy, can also help you when you are *behind* as well as leading. Forget the rather bleak prospect that you have lost the first set and are trailing in the second. Concentrate on winning each and every point, very much like the golfer who plays the course against par, one hole at a time, rather than worrying about what his opponent is doing.

Coasting shatters your concentration and disrupts your rhythm, and lost concentration and rhythm can well mean a lost match. Play to win as quickly as you can. Do not underrate *any* opponent. In this fascinating bat and ball sport, practically any team can lick (or lose to) any other team on a particular day.

3. *Purposeful Shots:* Since there are very few shots you can use to overwhelm or overpower the opposition, and it is extremely difficult to put a ball away, it is most important to hit as many *purposeful* shots as possible.

The proper platform tennis shot is one hit with a planned purpose behind it. Obviously, the ideal is to send the ball to a spot that results in a clean winner—or at least forces your opponent to

Bob Kingsbury, winner in 1972 with John Mangan in the National Doubles, displays the type of concentration, balance, and aggressiveness that are trademarks of the champions.

err. The next best thing is to hit a ball that causes the opposition to make a weak return, which allows you to put their ball away.

A defensive lob, if hit well, high, and deep, and with a purpose that exceeds merely returning the ball, can suddenly put you back on the offensive if your ball clears your opponents' paddles and forces them to retreat from the net in order to retrieve.

No matter what stroke you hit from *anywhere* in the court, make a concerted, concentrated effort to hit the ball with a winning purpose behind it. Probably the best way to summarize this idea is to suggest that you discipline yourself never (well, hardly ever) to hit a *non-thinking shot*. Think *where* you will hit the ball (prior to making your shot) and *why* you are employing this particular strategy. What do you hope to accomplish? Do not just blindly "clobber" the ball as hard as you can with the hope it will somehow go through your opponents for a lucky winner. The odds are definitely against you.

4. *Playing the Percentages:* This old adage holds true probably more in platform tennis than any other racquet game.

When there is no opening in your opponents' wall of defense there is no percentage in going down the alley. The "percentage shot" is low and down the middle where there is always a chance for your ball to go between them.

Whenever there is an obvious opening in the opposition's side of the court, don't be "cute" and hit for the outside of the back line or the alley. Place the ball beyond their reach, but still well within the boundary line of safety. Leave a margin. Why try to make an easy putaway a sensational shot? Play the shot that pays the big dividend, but involves the smallest risk. In other words, play the percentages.

5. *Bend Your Knees:* One of the fundamentals of hitting any ball with a racquet is: *Get down to the level of the ball.*

The majority of the balls you will have to hit will *not* conveniently bounce waist high. They will usually be balls that bounce no higher than your kneecaps, and frequently lower.

If you do not bend your knees, the natural tendency will be to hit up, and many of your balls will soar out of court.

By bending your knees you will be able to take a normal, proper stroke—the same grooved swing you take with a ball that bounces waist high.

There are other advantages to being in a crouched position on all shots, and especially when at net or waiting for a return of service. Bending the knees will help you to spring quickly in any direction necessary. Your whole body becomes a coiled spring. In addition, bending the knees helps you to relax, and that means you will not tire as quickly.

6. *The Playing Surface:* Remember that the surface of the playing deck, if it is proper, is extremely abrasive, and you will not be able to "slide" into your shots. It is necessary to give this warning, since I have seen many beginners attempt to slip into their ground strokes, the way they are used to doing on a tennis court. Watch out! The "no skid" surface can send one head over heels, and painful strawberries out of season are the result.

So, rather than slide, take two or three "baby steps" in order to get in proper hitting position. You will be there just as quickly and in a much healthier condition.

This abrasive playing surface also makes an exaggerated "wristy" slice shot *very* effective, as the ball really grabs the rough deck and "backs up"—to the surprise of the opponents.

7. *Concentration:* All non-contact games demand concentration on the part of the competitors; and this is especially true of racquet sports. Many an apparent victory has slipped away because one of the players lost his concentration.

In contact sports such as football when a participant is angered he can assuage his temper by making a vicious block or tackle. In tennis, or platform tennis, if you try to take it out on the ball you are well on your way to losing.

Usually the platform tennis gallery will be located within just a few feet of the screening surrounding the court. Many of the spectators will be wearing loud, contrasting colors, and some will be moving about during play. Such diversion can be most disconcerting to a competitor unless he concentrates *solely* on winning the match he is playing.

In tournament play you should be like a racing horse charging down the home stretch. Your concentration will provide you with the "blinkers" that shut out every distraction.

The next time you watch the better players during a platform tennis tournament, study them from the standpoint of their powers of concentration. Most of them will appear relaxed, hav-

The author is shown returning a low backhand as the ball re-bounds off the screen. Although forced into a rather awkward position, his body is sideways to the net, legs are bent, and the paddle face is open so that sufficient height will be given the ball to make sure it travels over the net.

The ballet-like acrobatics shown above by Al Collins, the south-paw, and Bob Kingsbury, is typical of what frequently occurs during a lengthy rally. Staying out of your partner's way takes almost as much skill as covering your half of the court against opponents' shots.

ing fun, and immensely enjoying the competition. Some will even smile and joke with the spectators.

The majority of the time, however, this frivolity is a veneer—a way of releasing tension. Beneath the surface there is a seriousness, a singleness of purpose, and a burning desire to win. Once a rally begins, or a key point is played, note that they instantly become oblivious to everything and everybody around them except the orange ball and winning the point.

The power of concentration, which acts as a tether on one's emotions and anger, is, indeed, every bit as important as sound ground strokes, a steady service, or fast reflexes at net. As a matter of fact, the ability to concentrate will help you to attain and retain all these attributes.

8. *Sportsmanship:* Platform tennis, perhaps even more than lawn tennis, is played by *gentlemen* (and *ladies*). The weekend players, whether they be avid competitors or ardent "just-for-fun" paddlers, are more often than not successful business and professional people—*amateurs* in the purest sense.

There is no "free list" for paddles, no expenses are ever paid by a tournament committee to lure the better performers. It is strictly a weekend avocation and a marvelous form of recreation and exercise during the cold wintry months.

Without exception, therefore, platform tennis is played between friends and sportsmen. Competitive play is no less intense or exciting when compared with any other racquet sport. But, when a match is over, no matter how heart-rending the final score, the foursomes shake hands and join one another for post-game socializing. There can be no griping or excuses—just lively discussions and warm camaraderie. There is no place for the "sorehead," the fellow who "calls them close," or the individual who always has an excuse. This prevailing sportsmanship is one of the great and unique features of the game of platform tennis. And may it remain that way!

CHAPTER 16

Attire and Equipment

Clothing: While the male players in the 30's wore fairly formal tennis attire (some even competed in sports coats and hats), the trend with platform tennis garb today is definitely toward the casual. Flamboyant multi-color sweaters, baggy flannel, corduroy, or khaki trousers, or stretch pants are "in" these days. Loud collored patches, such as hearts sewn on the pants, add to the fun.

The women play either in sweaters and skirts with woolen leotards, or stretch pants with matching jackets, or slacks. On many occasions a women's or mixed doubles event can look more like a fashion show than a sports event.

Whatever you decide to wear, no matter how loud and contrasting the colors, the most important aspect of your clothing is that it be warm and comfortable. Keep it in mind that you will frequently be playing when the thermometer shivers in the teens or even lower. Despite the cold you will, in time, probably perspire. So you don't want to be wearing anything that clings to you too tightly or begins to droop when it becomes wet.

It is advisable to bring along a dry change of clothes for after play, if there are facilities. There is no comfort in sitting around the club house in a wet shirt or sweater.

Equipment: Paddles and balls can be purchased from most leading sporting goods stores; *e.g.,* Feron's or Abercrombie's in New York City, or from your local club professional. If he stocks them, he should be supported.

In selecting a paddle, look for a comfortable grip and good balance. Most manufacturers offer paddles specially constructed for men or women. For example, the weight and grip of the Marcraft "Autograph" model was designed for the average male player, while the "Bantam" model—which is lighter and has a smaller handle grip—is more suitable for women.

Several companies have been recognized and approved by the American Platform Tennis Association as being manufacturers of official, quality paddles:

1. General Sportcraft Co., Ltd.
2. F. L. Fiberglass
3. Vittert
4. Marcraft
5. Dalton

These paddles are oval in shape and consist of a perforated surface. The head is approximately the same size as a tennis racquet and the material most frequently used is rock maple—occasionally aluminum and fiberglass. Paddles weigh between 15 and 17 ounces—the lighter ones are usually employed by women and the heavier by men. Most paddles are 17″ long and as the height of the net at its center is 34″, one can verify the exact height by merely standing two paddles on end.

Paddles range in price from $15.00 to $32.00 and a good paddle should last a long time with a minimum of care. Be sure to wipe off the surface after playing. Inasmuch as it picks up moisture, it is a good idea to keep the paddle covered with a paddle cover when not in use. Moisture can seep into the wood via the holes. The lacquered finish will wear with play but can be refinished. Merely sand lightly to a "feather edge," or use lacquer remover. Then apply a "sealer" and let dry overnight. Rub down with fine grit sandpaper, followed by two coats of lacquer 24 hours apart. The paddle should always be stored in a cool place, away from extremes of temperature. Any sporting goods store can apply a new leather grip at very modest cost.

Sportcraft, Vittert and Bullet currently make the balls, which sell for about $1 apiece. The ball is made of hard sponge rubber and is slightly smaller in diameter than a tennis ball. It is covered with bright orange or yellow flocking material.

Some players like to wear gloves to keep their hands warm during winter play as well as to provide a firm, sure grip on the paddle handle. Sportcraft, Vittert and Sports Accessories, Inc., manufacture and distribute paddle gloves.

Pro-Keds have developed a new platform tennis shoe which is both comfortable and durable. The gritty surface on the courts can be very rough on a regular pair of rubber-soled tennis shoes.

While most paddlers merely "do their thing" when it comes to playing attire, there has been a trend in recent years toward comfortable, stylized, functional clothes. Challe and R. C. Sportswear manufacture a line of paddle sweaters, slacks and shirts. Warmup suits are also becoming quite popular.

One of the attractions of taking up paddle, however, is the relatively nominal investment required to start you on your way. Balls last just about as long as tennis balls, paddles last practically forever and playing garb is very much like the same clothing you wear casually around your home or backyard.

CHAPTER 17

It's a New Game

The game of platform tennis has changed considerably in the last few years. There are two reasons for this change:

1. Younger athletes have become interested in the rapidly growing, popular winter sport and,

2. Many of these youthful converts have played a good deal of squash.

The top platform tennis players today, consequently, tend to be more *aggressive* and agile than their predecessors. They are not content to wait for their opponents to err. They also have a thorough understanding of the screens, and practically *any* ball is, in their minds, "gettable." It is not uncommon these days to see all four players at net simultaneously with volleying exchanges going back and forth more like a ping pong rally. This is a more offensive and bolder style of play than was conceived by the early promoters of the game.

And as the game has evolved, so have the players. For many years a rumor was circulated to the effect you had to be at least 40 years old to be a national champion, or a leading contender.

The rationale used to substantiate this theory was that platform tennis took a great deal of patience and tenacity. Overwhelming power and youthful zeal served no particular purpose. Only a person who had a mature outlook, the sagacity and good judgment that can come only with experience—the thinking approach —could be properly equipped, physically and emotionally, to become a champion platform tennis player.

This belief contained some truth, but the real reason it seemed to hold true for so many years was because younger players did not become enamored of the game until fairly recently. The "oldsters" had the sport pretty much to themselves while the youngsters took up squash, indoor tennis, or skiing.

Certainly patience and tenacity are important when it comes to playing competitive platform tennis, but just as important are agility, speed of foot, fast reflexes, a burning desire to win, stamina, and all the other qualities one associates with athletic youth.

I predict that within the next ten years a team that annexes the national doubles diadem will be in its early twenties—perhaps even teenagers! In the immediate future a great many school and college graduates will be taking up "our favorite sport" at an early age in lieu of other winter exercise. They will quickly find out that power alone cannot produce winning platform tennis, and when they do, watch out!

This does *not* mean there will be no room or place in the future for the "middle aged" athlete. Many a forty- or fifty-year-old team has beaten and will continue to beat the youthful upstart combination. I am merely pointing out what appears to be an inevitable trend toward younger champions, and there is no way to prevent the youngsters from becoming interested in platform tennis instead of other sports. The game's innate appeal is there.

As a matter of fact, we parents should encourage our children at an early age to play platform tennis. Most of them, I suspect, want to play, but find it impossible to get on the court during weekends. The grownups have every hour reserved.

Alumni (and alumnae) should suggest to their school and college alma maters that they install platform tennis courts. The squash coaches would probably protest at first, but these same coaches, usually, are also the tennis instructors—and certainly the strokes and play of platform tennis are more akin to tennis than to squash. Within the decade I would not be at all surprised to see the game played competitively between schools and colleges. It is a "natural." A Metropaddle intercollegiate league was started in 1976. Penn State and N.Y.U. each have installed six courts.

In addition to the APTA-sponsored national men's, women's, and mixed doubles championships, there has also been a national senior men's doubles tournament (age 50 or over) since 1957. A national boys' doubles tourney (age 20 or younger) was inaugurated in 1963, again part and parcel of the youth movement. There is also a senior veterans championship for men 60 years and over as well as a national 45s.

This broad base of activity and participation points up a very significant fact concerning platform tennis. The game is growing at a bewildering rate. Nationwide publicity is spreading the pleasures of platform tennis to the far-flung corners of the United States. The number of courts is multiplying at a fantastic rate.

It is interesting, as well as gratifying, to note that a leading advertising agency chose a platform tennis court as the site for an ad which depicts the "type" of person who uses their client's cognac.

Leaning across the net is a very suave, intelligent and auspicious-looking man, and snuggled up behind him is a most attractive, obviously highly-bred female model. Their demeanor, appearance, and attire make them realistic and plausible platform tennists. The theme of the advertisement, of course, is that discriminating, successful people enjoy the elegance of Hennessy cognac.

This full-color add appeared in many nationally distributed, widely-read publications and undoubtedly aroused the interest of racquet-wielders throughout the country . . . as well as cognac drinkers.

As the game continues to grow and expands into new areas, peripheral by-products will be created and distributed. Platform tennis clothing will inevitably be designed, paddles and balls will be improved, and perhaps even prefabricated courts that "anyone" can erect will be sold. A woman in Rye, New York, Marilyn Gerrish, has a thriving business going for her; she designs paddle racquet covers!

CHAPTER 18

Implementing a Successful Platform Tennis Program

Leslie C. Overlock

No matter how contagious a sport platform tennis may be, it still takes an *organized* program to put it over when new courts are installed. The following suggestions are written primarily for the Platform Tennis Chairman at a club (located in cold weather area) where two or more courts have just recently been erected. The identical procedures, however, hold true where courts are installed in city parks, at condominiums, in schools and colleges, at resorts or hotels, or even at a service base in, say, Nome, Alaska. Someone has to see that a program is developed to encourage participation. It is a very rewarding assignment; once the program is implemented and under way it will grow and expand almost automatically because of the game's great and broad attractions.

Platform Tennis Committee

It is important for the new chairman to select eight to ten committee members—preferably husband-wife combinations— who will inject their enthusiasm and energies into the "paddle program" for the entire season. Because the club is located in a cold weather region, the first meeting for the committee should take place no later than the middle of August, since play traditionally commences around the latter part of October. Well before the official kick-off of the season, a schedule of events and tournaments should be distributed to the membership.

Inaugural Exhibition

To help assure a propitious start-up, an inaugural exhibition–clinic given by four first-rate players is desirable. The tyros and totally unknowing members will see first hand how the game should be played. These exhibitions, if properly promoted and performed, are a marvelous way to engender enthusiasm and encourage participation among the members of any group.

Tournaments—and Other Events

At the committee meeting in August, a list of tournaments for the entire season should be planned. Care should be taken that these do not conflict with other invitation tourneys to be staged at near-by clubs. Assign a specific committee chairman for each event. Some of the following "friendly" club tournaments and events should be considered for any paddle program:

Mixed Member—Member Scrambles

This is an ideal event to kick off the new season. Anyone interested in playing the game can participate and have fun in this handicap type tournament. Players (male and female) are classified or ranked by the committee chairman "A" to "C," and the best (A) men are matched up with the weakest (C) women and vice versa. The entries are then carefully seeded so that the stronger teams do not meet each other in the early rounds.

To further increase interest and participation it is worthwhile to have both *Consolation* (all first round losers) and, when there are many entries, *Reprieve* (those teams eliminated in the second round) Championships.

The most successful handicapping method being employed to date is the so-called "Sliding Zero-to-Six System." Each team is carefully rated from zero (like scratch golfers, these are the toughest teams), two, four or six, with six being the weakest.

If the team is rated, say, six, this means they can, at their own choice and when it is most timely during the match (although they must announce to their opponents that they are taking their points *before* a game begins), decide *when* they wish to take their six points—which is tantamount to one and one-half games.

For example, if a six-rated team is vying against a two-rated team, the six or underdog combination can award itself four points (the difference between the two teams)—whenever they feel it will mean the most to them. Only the team with the higher handicap can decide when to use its points. If this team happens to be leading in the first set five games to four, obviously they will then take their four points, which means they automatically win the first set 6-4.

Now comes the great equalizing aspect of this type of handicapping. At the end of the first set, the winning team receives two fewer points for the next set. In the above illustration, the underdog team won the first set, and, therefore, has only two points to utilize in the second. If the favored (two-rated team) had won the first set, in spite of having to "give away" four points to the opposition, they would have to award six points during the second set. The same "sliding handicap" system would also hold true if a third or deciding set should be required.

It is truly amazing how well this system works, and it precipitates a great deal of fun and many close, exciting matches. It is obviously very important that the players and the teams be rated by a person(s) who is quite familiar with the players' games.

Mixed Member-Guest
This is usualy staged during the post-holiday "dog days" of January when people have recuperated sufficiently from Christmas and New Year's and are ready for a social–athletic weekend. In this format, club members invite partners from other clubs. This is usually a straight (no handicap) tourney, but Consolation and Reprieve matches

assure broad participation and adequate exercise for everyone.

Usually an integral and pleasant part of this tournament is the Saturday night dinner dance at the club. This enhances the conviviality of the event, and also enriches club revenues. (One club in Connecticut, which has had platform tennis courts for only three years, recently made a study of the financial impact of the game on their club revenues. Much to the pleasant surprise of everyone, they discovered that 68% of the income generated during the slow months of October through March was directly attributable to platform tennis).

Men's Member-Guest

Same as mixed doubles, except the girls spend the weekend watching and rooting for their husbands. Cocktail parties and a club dinner dance enhance the camaraderie of such a tournament.

Club Championships

These are usually held toward the end of the season, with the Ladies' played during the week and the Men's over a weekend. Plaques should be purchased for either the clubhouse or warming hut, and the names of the winning teams inscribed on them with the appropriate year. Photographs of the finalists can be framed and hung to enhance the prestige and tradition of these events.

The Husband-Wife Club Championship

Otherwise humorously dubbed "The Divorce Open," or "The Longest Weekend," this tournament can be the most fun of all, despite its being a great test of even the happiest marriages. But in spite of the glares, the tears, and moments of strained silence, serious marital break-ups have not been reported. The winning combination can "stand tall" with the knowledge that they have truly earned their trophies.

Friday Night Paddle Parties
At least once a month during the winter, couples who have been bitten by the platform tennis bug should be encouraged to stage Friday night round robin events. If the number of couples exceeds eight, it is best to divide the teams into two or more flights. Each team plays, say, eight games against all the other combinations in its group. The teams with the greatest number of games for their respective flights, then meet and play a one set final.

An important part of such social competition is an open-fire barbecue or cookout with an abundant supply of liquid refreshment both hot and cold. Such an evening can be inexpensive, and a marvelous way to end up a hard week and start a fun weekend.

Junior Championships
If the kids (18 and under) at the club ever have an opportunity to play (their parents usually have the courts reserved), they too should be encouraged to compete in a club championship against their own age group.

The ideal time to have this event—if eight or more teams can be fielded—is during Christmas or midwinter holidays when they are on vacation and can play during the week.

Parent-Child Tournaments
This event is always enjoyable, and a special treat for the children. It is best to schedule it during the holidays when the kids are home and available.

Special Club Invitationals
Many clubs have become regular stopovers for the better men and women players during the season. The dates selected for invitation tournaments should fall on approxi-

mately the same weekend each year—in other words, they become traditional events.

The teams invited are frequently the best players available, and watching them play affords club members the opportunity of viewing the game as performed by "experts." Such events arouse the interest of the entire club, and improved play invariably occurs because the novices attempt to emulate the "pros." Quite often a major social function is scheduled around such an event and the visiting players attend. During the evening the inevitable question is asked of the competitors by the members: "Say, how would you like to play with me in our Member-Guest Tournament?"

Ladies' Day

One morning a week—usually Wednesdays—should be designated strictly for the ladies. Round robin competition, coffee and donuts, perhaps even a lunch, provide the girls with a pleasant and healthy mid-week outlet.

Because of this concession to the distaffers, most clubs give preference on Saturday and Sunday mornings to the hard-working, commuting businessmen.

Junior Clinics

Several clubs have inaugurated a development program for the youngsters who much too rarely get the opportunity to play. A few of the better male players in these clubs have scheduled early Saturday morning 8:00 to 9:00 o'clock clinics for interested adolescents in the age bracket of 10 to 16. They have been tremendously successful and well attended.

Family Days

As platform tennis becomes more and more popular, Sunday afternoons from 2 until 5 are frequently reserved strictly for family play. This is a wonderful idea since it is, indeed, a fabulous family-participation sport. It also provides the youngsters with another opportunity to improve.

Inter-Club League Matches

As platform tennis expands to neighboring clubs, ladies' and men's inter-club rivalries should develop and be encouraged. These are friendly team matches that occur during the season and usually involve a "home" and "away" match against each club. Such reciprocity affords everyone the opportunity of entertaining each other's team and enjoying each other's club facilities.

Miscellaneous

All club final round matches for *all* tournaments should be umpired. This officiating lends a good deal of stature to the event, and is greatly appreciated by players and spectators.

Every institution, whether it be a club, resort, or condominium, should automatically join the American Platform Tennis Association just as soon as the courts are installed. By joining, they will be kept abreast of the latest happenings in the sport, receive tournament notices, and then feel part of the game.

A bulletin board strictly for platform tennis should be acquired and displayed in an obvious place either in the clubhouse or warming hut. Coming events, sign-up sheets for tournaments, playing rules, announcements, etc., will be posted for members. It is a good way to communicate with the players and keep the action going.

Tournaments should be publicized at least three weeks in advance of the date, and the particular chairman of the event must be prepared to make many phone calls to remind and encourage the players to participate.

Entry fees for all these tournaments and events mentioned above should be established at a modest rate, but should also be adequate to cover the cost of balls, prizes, refreshments and whatever. More elaborate optional events that are part of a tournament (*e.g.*, a formal dinner dance) are charged separately.

It is always worthwhile to present some sort of prizes for tournaments. Even the rather inconsequential Ladies' Day round robin should offer recognition to the winners—even if only with something as simple as a few new balls. The more prestigious championships should offer functional prizes and have the particular event engraved on them.

Monies for such "spoils" can be obtained either at the beginning or close of the season by soliciting the members to contribute to a "Platform Tennis Prize Fund." Donations are completely voluntary, but if a person who hasn't contributed happens to win one of the tournaments, he should not receive the trophy. This system has proved successful in raising funds.

Capital for New Courts

A wooden platform tennis court presently runs around $12,500 with lights—a metal court about $20,000. If a club is not able to pay for them out of capital expenditures, financial commitments must be obtained directly from the members. The fairest method of obtaining capital is to solicit only those members who are interested in playing and who will utilize the courts, rather than arbitrarily assessing all of the membership.

Some clubs have done this by forming a *separate* platform tennis membership, while others have solicited "up front pledges" from families most interested in a paddle program.

Usually a long-range commitment is more successful than a large chunk of money sought immediately. Fifty families might be willing and able to contribute $200 each, but 100 families might be more willing to contribute $50 a year for three years. The former way provides $10,000, the latter $15,000.

Keep in mind that it is always wise, whenever possible, to install a minimum of two courts. One court can frequently discourage people from taking up the game because of the difficulty in getting a reserved time. Two courts, set side by side or end to end, breed camaraderie and the amenities that are so much a part of this game. A warming hut is highly desirable.

Installation of Courts

There is a definite procedure to be employed when consideration is being given to the installation of platform tennis courts.

It is important that thought be given to the determination of a proper site. First, the area selected should be aesthetically appropriate. Consideration must also be given to the convenience factor; how far from the clubhouse and the parking lot? Since lights for night play are really and truly a must, selecting a site within close proximity to a power source is important. Also, how accessible will the area be in case of a heavy snowfall? The area should be large enough to accommodate additional courts as well as a warming hut. Also the site chosen should be one that is accessible for ease of construction, and if the area is a residential one, thought should be given to any potential problems and complaints that could arise from neighbors.

After the site has been determined, it is important to obtain bids from bona fide contractors who are *experienced* in platform tennis courts construction. Sometimes clubs and institutions desiring courts engage a local carpenter and live to regret it.

There is an art to building a good platform tennis facility and only those concerns who have experienced crews can do it properly. Don't always award the contract to the lowest bidder either; reliability and performance have their compensations.

After a particular method of financing the courts has been resolved, the new court-owner-to-be should apply for a building permit if this is required. Then be sure to stipulate a completion date for construction with your contractor and give the builder as much lead time as possible.

By adopting the above suggestions, and adding your own individual, novel ideas, you should be well on your way to the successful implementation of a platform tennis program.

CHAPTER 19

Potentials
of the Game

Schools and Colleges

Just think of all those learning institutions located in the northern climes that have a prodigious number of tennis courts for a season that lasts all of two months—April and May and perhaps a few weeks in the fall. What a waste! Platform tennis courts, on the other hand, could be utilized for a minimum of 6 months. In addition, many schools and colleges that have traditionally been all male have now become coeducational. The co-eds find themselves with meager athletic facilities. Wouldn't platform tennis be the perfect game for them?

If Harvard should install four courts, Yale and Princeton would almost immediately erect six and eight respectively. I can envision avid intercollegiate competition taking place with the top event being *mixed* doubles. Why not?

While athletic directors have to spend much of their time building up a strong football team to placate the old grads, most of them are chiefly concerned with ways of cajoling the majority of the students to participate in some—or any—sports activity at all. Intra-mural, non-varsity athletic programs for the "unnatural" athletes are really what they are dedicated to establishing. Broad participation is the aim.

Certainly platform tennis is the ideal game for the non-athletic as well as the natural athlete. The expense of a coach is not necessary, since it is the only racquet game I know of where a person can pick up a paddle and have fun (without becoming totally frustrated) from practically the first moment on.

My fondest dream is to be sitting one day in the bleachers watching the finals of the U.S. Intercollegiate Platform Tennis Doubles Championship. Wouldn't that be great! And I suspect the complexion and style of the game will have changed considerably. The play will undoubtedly be far more aggressive, with more of a premium on lightning-like reflexes, speed of foot, and a greater majority of hard-hit shots off the wires.

And then when they are graduated from their respective academic institutions and go out into the business or professional world, they will obviously take their sport with them, and Lord help the club they join if "paddle" is not one of its leisure-time activities!

Resorts

Certainly resorts, including lavish hotels and motels, ski areas, hunting lodges, etc., represent a vast potential market for the introduction of the game as an added facility. With shorter work weeks and more time for travel, sport and fun, these resorts will inevitably be competing for a greater portion of the dollars spent by people in "pursuit of happiness." The owners of these holiday paradises and hostelries have come to the realization that they not only should, but must offer their guests a great deal more than delectable viands, clean sheets and color TV. Conveniences, social activities and recreational facilities are no longer additional "fringes"—they are absolute necessities if the resorts are to attract the trade.

Many owners and managers now are beginning to learn that they must remain open the year around in order to show a profit. Ski resorts are, therefore, attempting to promote themselves as summertime, fun places to stay in and the traditional warm-weather vacation spots are winterizing their rooms and trying to become winter "wonderlands."

Platform tennis is certainly one facility that, properly introduced and promoted, will lure people to a particular place over some others. The decade of the seventies should show a swing of the pendulum back toward the family and an eagerness to return to genteel, participation sports. The violence of football, the sedentary state of spectating, the slowness and "apartness" associated with golf, the ennui of swimming, the continuing growth of regular tennis, and an increasing concern for physical fitness and healthy exercise should all be important factors in making platform tennis a welcome pastime during the next few years.

The small space required for a court is also appealing to resort owners who have to figure every acre (just as supermarket managers compute their shelf space) as revenue-producing units with which to outdo and outsell their competition. Three indoor tennis courts, plus the structure, will cost anywhere from $300,000 to $450,000. Three "paddle" courts that offer the outdoor lovers clean air and refreshing, healthful exercise can be erected for $40,000 to $60,000—and still mean substantial new-found revenues.

In addition, little or no maintenance is required to keep the courts in top playing condition—less than five percent upkeep annually. With ever-increasing labor costs, platform tennis courts certainly involve a great deal less servicing than either swimming pools or tennis courts.

Although I may be accused of being prejudiced, I truly believe there is no better recreational facility for a resort, motel or hotel to offer visitors. The installation of platform tennis courts, accompanied by a well-planned program and some publicity, can certainly mean surefire, increasing profits to the establishment— with a minimum investment required.

Municipalities

Most cities throughout the country are presently concerned with two very basic and omnipresent problems: 1) the young people in their streets, many of whom seem to be rather apathetic toward recreation and healthful physical exercise and 2) a shrinking percentage of the city budget being allotted to recreation at a time when funds are most needed.

Even though the majority of those responsible are concerned individuals, they have, by circumstance and necessity, found that public recreational facilities ought to be at least self-sustaining. It would be wonderful if the public swimming pool, golf course, and tennis courts could be free to all citizens, but with ever-increasing costs this is no longer possible.

Any city or town in the U.S.A. would find it hard to select a more perfect facility than platform tennis courts. They would help to keep the parks open and utilized the year around. The lights for night play would make the parks safer during the evenings. The courts require very little space and a minimum amount of maintenance. No other racquet and ball sport offers richer rewards for family participation during long winter evenings.

When funds have been unavailable in the city budget, some communities have screened their citizens as to the amount of interest they might have in platform tennis. Nominal financial commitments have been obtained in the form of $25- to $50-per-season family memberships, thereby making it possible to obtain the required balance from a local bank.

Many people concerned with their personal physical fitness and well-being will be more than willing to pledge a reasonable sum each season for the joys of this game, and it doesn't take too many commitments to have enough to afford paddle courts.

Figuring fifty families per court, a couple of hundred families can easily obtain 3 to 4 courts—and a full-fledged platform tennis program is off the ground, paid for and supported by the people who utilize and enjoy the facility.

Country Clubs

The majority of private golf and tennis clubs today find themselves unhappy victims of the current depressed economy. Many of their members have resigned because they can no longer afford to belong. Other members who continue to belong have had to cut back drastically on their club participation.

Increased labor costs, combined with the difficulty of being able to hire good, reliable labor at any price has, when added to the other problems, really put the squeeze on innumerable private clubs throughout the nation.

What is the solution for these clubs? How are they ever going to survive? The answer is easy and inexpensive—wintertime Platform Tennis!

Increased club usage means increased revenues that more than offset the additional expenses involved in keeping the club facilities open.

If need be, a separate, winter platform tennis membership can be instituted at a nominal rate.

Platform tennis is unique from the standpoint that practically anyone—young or old—can have fun playing it while learning. People who cannot play tennis become completely addicted.

The deck is 30' x 60', or one-quarter the area of a regulation tennis court. When space is at premium, portable decks can be installed in the fall right over the tennis courts, and dismantled and stored away in the spring.

As the game continues to expand into new areas, and many new players are exposed to its delights, undoubtedly more team matches will be instigated—thus creating an increased amount of activity at the clubs. Women, especially, will find themselves using the club facilities during the week with greater frequency.

For approximately $12,500 per court, a club will be investing in recreational facilities that mean increased club usage, greater revenues, and an attractive, new form of exercise that the majority of the membership will use and enjoy.

Real Estate Development Communities

Many corporations in the years ahead intend to invest heavily in land and in the development of recreational, leisure-oriented communities. Their marketing efforts will be slanted toward convenience, the second home, or "own your own home and rent it out when you are not using it." Pollution-free air, the serene life, carefree days of fun and recreation, will be the copywriters' favorite themes.

With shorter work weeks, increased leisure hours and early retirement, such idyllic meccas will fill a great need and stir the imagination. Add concern for health and physical fitness and the installation of platform tennis courts makes a good deal of sense.

The architects and planners of these developments from their inception wouldn't think of excluding such basic facilities as tennis courts, a swimming pool, perhaps a golf course, and shuffle-board or the like for the elderly.

If these same planners can be familiarized with platform tennis, many most assuredly would include courts in the original plans. Why? Again, the courts consume little valuable space, require a small investment and minimum of maintenance, and can and will be used by families of all ages, and in almost any kind of weather. What other form of recreation offers so much?

Rooftops

The only valuable unutilized space in crowded major cities across the country nowadays is rooftops. In-town city dwellers could find enjoyment and a healthy release during the evening hours or on weekends by joining a club that offers roof-top platform tennis. Platform tennis courts can *usually be* squeezed in anywhere, and they offer a possible money maker for the investors. There is a great future for commercial platform tennis centers.

Corporate Headquarters

Company morale is a key concern for present-day American businesses. A highly organized recreational program for employees, from the plant sweeper on up, is a primary objective of many firms. Many establishments across the country have made the exodus to suburbia where land is plentiful and the employees no longer have to spend a great deal of their day commuting to work. Appealing and well-planned recreational programs and facilities breed a feeling of esprit and "belonging." They also keep the employees in reasonably good physical condition.

Platform tennis is the perfect facility to offer these employees. Industrial leagues could quickly become a reality and popular.

Other places where platform tennis can be played are: campmobile and trailer sites, private homes, YMCAs and YWCAs, hospitals and nursing homes, driving ranges and pitch and putt golf courses, prisons, health spas and sanatoriums, beach clubs, amusement parks, day camps, and over swimming pools. They can also become an added activity for indoor tennis clubs, and neighborhood semi-private sports complexes.

Platform tennis truly is a sport with broad appeal for everyone. It should become *The Game* in the forthcoming decade.

CHAPTER 20

Platform Tennis Myths

For close to a half century, since its inception, platform tennis has been a victim of several persistent misconceptions. These myths have done much to impede the growth and widespread popularity of the game. The time has come to dispel them!

Myth # 1: *Platform tennis is only a cold-weather sport.* This impression is utter nonsense and has been perpetuated only because the game was originally invented to be a "between seasons" activity. Many of the more traditional paddlers argue that the ball gets too hot and, therefore, too lively when the temperature rises to over 65 degrees. "It's almost impossible to put it away," they claim. It has also been said that the abrasive decking is quite uncomfortable on the feet and the surrounding chicken-wire screening contains and reflects the heat.

Isn't it rather ridiculous that it has to be around 20 to 25 degrees in order to make a racquet-and-ball sport enjoyable? The truth of the matter is that platform tennis is an all-season sport to be played and enjoyed in any kind of weather. It honestly is no more enervating to play platform tennis on an elevated deck in the summer than tennis on an asphalt or cement court. As a matter of fact, it is several degrees *cooler,* because the playing surface is up off the ground.

I suspect there are millions of Americans who, although they don't openly admit it, are rapidly becoming disenchanted with tennis. They have taken plenty of lessons from the club professional, but do not seem to be improving much. They would certainly gain a great deal more personal satisfaction and, therefore, fun if they took up paddle. I predict platform tennis will one day soon be played the year around and many current fair tennis players will convert and become very good paddlers.

Myth # 2: *Platform tennis ruins one's tennis game.* Admittedly, there is a totally different "feel" between hitting a tennis ball with a strung racquet and making contact with the perforated wooden or aluminum paddles against the heavy, sponge-rubber ball. It would be rather difficult to play both of these sports on the same day, but a person who can play paddle and tennis would have no trouble participating in these games on alternating days. After all, the basic strokes are identical. Squash, paddleball and racquetball are all hit with a loose wrist and a short, whiplike swing. Platform tennis, on the other hand, employs the same flowing, long (slightly abbreviated) stroke, with a locked wrist.

The short distance between opponents does much to hone one's footwork and reflexes. The team controlling the net the majority of the time will usually win; so there is a premium on racquet work and volleying. As your opponents are but a scant few feet away, your reactions must be razor-sharp. If you decide to go back to the tennis court in the spring, you will find it difficult to believe you have the luxury of so much time between exchanges. The tennis court will seem huge! Your net game and sense of anticipation will be vastly improved.

The single serve of paddle will do much to help you put your first serve into play the majority of the time on the tennis court. Getting the first service in has become increasingly more important in top-flight tournament tennis—especially in doubles.

Finally, there is no better training ground for young children whose parents aspire for them to become future tennis champions than the platform tennis court. The kids can easily relate to the smallness of the court and can more readily learn the fundamental strokes and strategy of tennis on a paddle court. The only danger is that they just might decide they enjoy platform tennis more!

Myth # 3: *Platform tennis is not a bona-fide racquet sport.* I imagine this myth was promoted by purist tennis players who believe every other racquet-and-ball sport is a bastardized off-spring of lawn tennis. They have undoubtedly never tried seriously to play platform tennis.

While it is true paddle takes less skill and time to be able to play well enough to have fun, it is also a fact that the game is just as difficult to master as any sport. To become a champion requires a good deal of practice and adroit racquet work. Granted, legs and lungs are not the vital factors they are in tennis, but these are not the sole ingredients that make up a bona-fide sport. Ask any golfer. For that matter, our national pastime, baseball, does not take much stamina.

What constitutes a bona-fide racquet sport? My guess is: speed of foot, concentration, reflexes, shot-making, control of the ball and one's emotions, a repertoire of strokes, ball placement and determination. Certainly all these characteristics are required to become a platform tennis champion.

Myth # 4: *Platform tennis does not require professional instruction.* Too many courts have been installed recently where there has been no one to show people how to play platform tennis properly. There are presently very few professional teachers. The mere installation of courts does *not,* unfortunately, assure the instant popularity of the game. All too frequently, first-time players become frustrated because they do not have anyone to teach them how to hit the ball, where to hit it, and why certain strategies work while others don't.

Invariably a fine tennis player will employ tennis strokes and tennis strategy the first time he plays paddle. Unless someone corrects what he is doing wrong, he will, indeed, believe platform tennis is a rather silly game. He won't understand why he just can't blow his opponent off the court with an awesome display of power, or why he is having so much trouble getting his serve in. Playing the ball off the wires will forever remain a total mystery unless a capable instructor works with him.

The present lack of professional instruction is truly a shame, and I feel the game of platform tennis has undoubtedly lost many potentially fine paddlers because they were improperly initiated in the sport. It is very important, therefore, that interested tennis players try to obtain some kind of basic instruction right at the beginning. Exhibitions and clinics to inaugurate new courts do much to familiarize people with the correct shots and winning tactics unique to paddle. Eventually, as the game continues to spread, professional platform tennis instructors will become more prevalent, and that will do much to further popularize the game and raise the level of play.

Myth # 5: *Platform tennis frequently causes "tennis elbow."* Although it is true the heavier paddle and ball put more strain on a person's forearm and elbow at the moment of impact, it is equally a fact that a *properly* stroked ball is the greatest deterrent against the painful experience of tennis elbow. The platform tennis swing should be just as smooth and fluid as the tennis stroke. It is important to warm up sufficiently before actually starting to play. This is especially vital in paddle, since it is often played in cold, damp weather.

Snapped Achilles tendons, dislocated knees and backs can also occur on the platform tennis court—mainly because of the non-skid deck surface. Again, though, if one is careful and mindful of the dangers, such accidents need never happen.

I have always said that I will know the game has "arrived" when someone tells me he has just recovered from a severe case of "paddle elbow"!

There are other myths which really have no rationale or foundation. Tradition can often be a progress-impeding factor. When more and more people start playing and discovering the pleasures of the sport, however, these myths will be quickly shattered by the truths inherent in this wonderful game. What's the real truth? Platform tennis is a *great* racquet-and-ball sport to be played and enjoyed by anybody and everybody.

CHAPTER 21

Some Hazards of the Game

David W. Wilson, M.D.

There is no sport without hazards for its participants. Most serious platform tennis players can display a scar or two or remember an injury.

Sports medicine is becoming a specialty. Injuries are analyzed and equipment and playing surfaces are studied for safety. I make no pretense of being a specialist in sports injuries, and I am a pedestrian paddle addict. However, a number of repeated accidents and complaints swell my office records as each season attracts more and more fans to the sport. Reading what follows gives no guarantee that you will retain an intact skin or skeleton, but it may reduce the number of calls to your physician, especially on weekends.

The short, heavy paddle, the half-dead sponge-rubber ball, and the small court all become factors in the hazards that platform tennis players face.

Perhaps the most common complaint attributable to the game is a sore elbow, tennis elbow (lateral epicondylitis). Those who suffer from it need advice from a pro on the correct way to make their shots. Elbow pain primarily on backhand strokes can be enough to ruin the season. The forearm must be considered part of the paddle and the wrist held fixed on contact with the ball or the impact is transmitted up the forearm to the site of attachment of the forearm extensor muscles, a point of bone sharper in women than in men. The muscle and tendon fibers rub and become irritated if wrist movement is occurring at the time of impact. Weak or fatigued forearm muscles permit motion at the wrist on impact, and tennis elbow is then likely to occur.

ADVICE:

1. Stroke your backhand shots correctly.
2. Take it a little easy when beginning the season.
3. If your elbow gets sore, get a pro to help you correct your bad habits.

The short paddle can bring the hard, solid paddle head close to your own head. The metal band on the perimeter can make the paddle a fairly lethal weapon. New players who may well be skilled in tennis, squash, or badminton often lay open their eyebrows or forehead while attempting to return a close-in ball.

Some partners can be an even greater hazard in the heat of play. Avoiding slashing your partner is what many pages of this book are about. The size of the court and the speed of the action demand attention to the details of good team play, especially a loud, vocal communication between you and your partner.

ADVICE:

If you sustain a bad bruise, cold applications, ice or snow, may reduce the amount of swelling.

The court surface is unforgiving. It is hard. It is slip-proofed with a rough, sandy finish. There can be no decelerating slide to ease an abrupt change in direction as on most tennis courts. The screen is ever nearby to limit running room. Ankles and knees are therefore subjected to severe stresses. Unexpected risky stresses occur on a court where fragments of ice or snow remain uncleared.

ADVICE:

Wear footwear designed for the game.

Inspect the court for ice, protruding nails, varying heights of the deck boards, and defective screening.

A half-wet court may be slick from previous use of ice-melting salt. So test your footing.

The close play at net requires rapid-fire exchanges, full alertness and proper stance—with your paddle as the only available shield against fast balls returned to you. Unbreakable eyeglasses for those who must wear them can reduce the hazard from an unlucky direct hit.

As with every sport, time taken to warm up contributes not only to better performance, but to reducing potential injuries. Unused muscles tend to be tense, especially in the cold. The sudden stretching of a tight calf muscle at the end of a leap can surpass the elastic limits of the Achilles tendon. Such a rupture relegates the player to many months on the sidelines.

ADVICE:
> Bend from the waist, knees locked, to stretch leg tendons before playing.

Exercising increases the rate and depth of respiration. On a crisp, cold day mouth-breathing carries the unwarmed air into the throat and lungs. If their membranes are normal no adverse reaction other than a runny nose occurs. However, should you have a respiratory infection the added inflammation and secretions must be deemed a hazard.

ADVICE:
> Stick by fireside on such occasions.

The abrasive platform surface and its surrounding chicken-wire screen make falling and moving out of control the cause of many "paddle" battle scars. When you fall, roll like a ball player, or tumbler, in the direction of the fall. Many have had no training in this kind of rolling, and the court is no place to practice it.

An ungloved hand extended to break a fall may lose some layers of epidermis, and clothing over such bony prominences as elbows and knees can be reduced to shreds when you lose your footing. It is better to roll if you can. If you run out of court room, turn your side—or, better, your back—to the screening. There are two advantages: the impact will be less painful, and you can bounce back, as a boxer does off the ropes, to recover.

An outstretched arm to slow the impact against the screen is asking for a variety of game-ending hurts.

And don't forget or ignore frostbite. Rubbing snow on an affected area is medically obsolete. Prompt, gentle warming is the recommended first aid, with secondary medical treatment or advice to follow if necessary. Cold causes constriction of surface blood vessels, with mottling and pallor of skin. Exposed ears and fingers are most in danger. The player himself may not realize that frostbite has occurred to an ear tip. You can be a good friend to make him aware if you note the obvious change in skin color.

The foregoing is in no way to be construed as a deterrent from enjoying platform tennis. The fun and exhilaration derived from playing this game justify the hazards, many of which can be minimized by prior awareness.

CHAPTER 22

Singles

by *Gregg Brents**

Platform tennis players have neglected singles for too long. If singles had not been shelved in the 1930s, platform tennis would today be enjoying an even greater popularity explosion.

Recently there have been several attempts to resurrect the singles game, but for the most part they have failed to catch on. What is it that keeps most platform tennis players from taking the singles game seriously?

By analyzing the conventional singles game, we can easily discover why it has fallen from favor: The angles available to the player who is in control of the net make it virtually impossible for the opposing backcourt player to execute an aggressive game plan. By repeatedly using cross-court shots, first to one side screen and then to the other, the net player can send his opponent chasing the ball back and forth across the court. Thus the player who first gains control of the net (normally the server) will be practically unbeatable. Even in half-court singles, the player who does not have net position will be run ragged after the first few games, especially if the ball is heavy because of cold weather and thus "dies" on the side screen.

To prosper and continue to grow in popularity, platform tennis must have a workable singles game. All sports thrive on competition and challenge, and singles offers the one-to-one combat that both spectators and players find so exciting. Furthermore, a playable and exciting singles game will help platform tennis players solve their constant problem—rounding up four people for a match. (How many times have you heard people say, "Will I be

---

*Gregg Brents is a touring professional platform tennis player and is currently head professional at the Apple Platform Tennis Club in New York City.

able to get a game?" or "We'll have to cancel because we can't find a fourth.") Being able to arrange matches for only two players will go a long way to solving this problem. An attractive, enjoyable singles game will add immeasurably to the popularity of platform tennis.

John P. Ware wrote in *The Complete Book of Platform Tennis* that the birth of a sport often "just happens." Oddly enough, it "just happened" that the idea for a workable singles game hit me one morning. First, the thought seemed entirely too simple: what would happen if you were forced to hit the *back screen first*? My next step was to play out this idea on a sheet of paper with a sketch of the conventional court layout. (See diagram 1.) After simulating many points with my pencil and becoming more excited by the minute, I stopped in my tracks. This idea still seemed too easy—such a slight rule change. There must be a bevy of problems I had not even considered. After arriving at the club, I explained my idea to a friend who plays very little paddle. Since he was the only person around that early in the morning, he and I grabbed paddles and began experimenting by playing points. The idea really began to make good sense.

Let me first explain the basic rule of "Back Screen First" (the nickname I use for the game): After the serve, a ball that hits a side screen is a fair shot only if it has hit the back screen first. (Of course before it hits the back screen, the ball must have touched inside the boundaries of the court.) If the ball caroms into the side screen following a back-screen hit, it is played as a two-wire shot. Should the ball ever strike the side screen first (regardless of whether the ball touched fairly within the singles boundaries), the player hitting the ball loses the point. The only exception is the service, which, as in doubles, *may* touch the side screen first.

Immediate comments regarding "Back Screen First" by a few pros who played were that it was truly a lot of fun and definitely a good game. To date, I feel "Back Screen First" is the best solution to the "singles problem" for the following reasons:

1. It eliminates the extreme wide angles that have rendered the

original singles game all but obsolete by forcing players to hit "straight ahead."

2. It does not require a player to be in excellent physical condition. A small percentage of pros may be capable of covering the entire court in playing full-court singles, but what about Mr. and Mrs. Public?

3. It not only allows a player to reach virtually every ball, but also puts him in position to make an aggressive return shot.

4. It produces more lengthy rallies during points.

5. It enables a player to exercise a larger repertoire of shots.

6. It inevitably produces better players with all-round skills.

7. It does not require any physical modifications of existing boundary lines.

8. It creates exciting spectator appeal.

9. It does not require a psychological reorientation to playing doubles (which the half-court singles game does).

At this time, the only drawback to "Back Screen First" is that it eliminates the cross-court passing shot from the game. (Remember, you may *not* strike the side screen first except when serving.) Because the cross-court passing shot is an exciting one to watch and exhilarating to execute, let me offer two suggestions that have been made. First, if the ball lands *beyond the service line* during play, it may then be hit cross-court into the side screen, after touching within the singles boundaries. Second, a vertical line could be painted on the side screens within a few feet of the back corners (where the back and side screens meet). Any ball that strikes this line or beyond it on the side screen is fair. Either one of these suggestions will give singles players the advantages of "Back Screen First" without sacrificing cross-court shots to the side screen.

So the first step has been taken. We now have a game *everyone* can play and really enjoy. Perhaps time and play will decide upon what modifications or changes are needed. You may laughingly consider this just another version, but find a court and give it a fair chance. You may find yourself caught up in the game, then addicted to it, just as I am.

C. Michael O'Hearn, former National champion, is hitting down on a high bouncing ball from deep in the backhand corner. From the position of his paddle, it appears, because of the height of the ball, that he intends to hit a slice shot.

Mike's father, Charlie, first won the U.S. Doubles title twenty-eight years before his son.

CHAPTER 23

APTA
Official Rules of Platform Tennis

RULE 1

Dimensions and Terminology

The *court* is a rectangle 44′ long and 20′ wide, laid out on a surface with a playing area 60′ by 30′ which is enclosed by a *screen* 12′ high. The screen is held taut by a superstructure around the perimeter of the deck. Screens are made of 1″ hexagonal galvanized wire mesh.

The court is divided across the middle by a *net,* the ends of which are attached to *posts*. The posts are 37″ high and 18″ outside the court (acceptable tolerance ±6″). The height of the net at the posts is 37″ and at center is 34″. The net is held down taut and adjusted for height by a vertical *center strap* 2″ wide.

The lines at the ends of the court, parallel to the net, are called *baselines*. The lines at the sides of the court, perpendicular to the net, are called *sidelines*. Two feet inside the sidelines and running parallel to them for the length of the court are the *alley lines*. Twelve feet from the net on either side and running parallel to it from alley line to alley line are the *service* lines. The segments of the alley lines between the service lines and the net are called the *service* sidelines. The area between the net and the service lines is divided in half by a line perpendicular to them. This line is called the *center service line*. Each baseline is bisected by an imaginary extension of the center service line called the *center mark*. The center mark appears as a line 4″ long extending into the court at right angles to, and touching the baselines.

The area between the baseline and the service line is called the *backcourt*. The area between the service line and the net is called the *forecourt,* which in turn is divided into two *service courts,* left and right. The area between the side line and the alley line is called the *alley*.

All lines are customarily 2″ wide and all measurements are made to the outside of the lines from the net or the center of the center service line. This line is in both service courts and is itself centered on the imaginary center line of the court. All lines are within the court.

There is a space of 8′ between each baseline and the *back screen,* and a space of 5′ between each side line and the *side screen.* These spaces are part of the playing area, but they are not part of the court.

RULE 2

Court Fixtures

Court fixtures are the net, the posts, the cord (or metal cable) that holds up the net, the band across the top of the net, the center strap, the screens, the snow boards, the superstructure, the doors, the lighting poles and lights, and crossbeams or corner supports within the enclosure, and, when they are present, the umpire and his chair.

RULE 3

The Ball and the Paddle

The ball is a rubber ball with either orange or yellow flocking, conforming to APTA specifications for diameter, weight, bounce and other standards as set forth in Appendix A.

The paddle is 17″ in overall length with a playing area 10⅜″ long and a handle 6⅝″ long. The paddle is perforated with a number of ⅜″ holes. The surface of the paddle must be flat and the finish smooth. APTA paddle standards are set forth in Appendix B.

RULE 4

Use of Ball and Paddle

Only one ball shall be used continuously during each set unless otherwise specified by the tournament committee. Server may not substitute another ball during an unfinished set without the permission of tournament officials, nor may server hold two balls while serving.

A player may not carry a second paddle during play, although it is permissible to use both hands on the paddle and to switch the paddle from hand to hand in the course of play.

RULE 5

Doubles Only

Platform tennis customarily is played only as a game of *doubles,* with two players on each side. The side that is serving is called the *serving team,* and the other side is called the *receiving team.*

Although singles may be played for fun or practice, there are no singles tournament competitions—to date.

RULE 6

Choice of Sides and Service

The choice of sides and the right to serve first or to receive first is decided by toss, which is generally accomplished by spinning the paddle.

The team that does not toss has the right to call the toss. The team winning the toss has the following options:

(a) the right to serve first, in which case the other team has the right to choose from which end of the court to receive;

(b) the right to receive first, in which case the other

team has the right to choose from which end of the court to serve;

(c) the right to choose the end, in which case the other team has the right to elect to serve first or to receive first;

(d) the right to require the other team to make the first choice.

RULE 7

Server and Receiver

After the toss has been concluded, the teams take their places on opposite sides of the net. The member of the serving team who elects to serve first becomes the *server*. The member of the receiving team who elects to play the right court becomes the first *receiver*.

The server must deliver service from a position behind the baseline and between the center mark and the sideline, diagonally crosscourt from the receiver.

The receiver may stand wherever he pleases on his own side of the net, on or off the court. Likewise the server's partner and the receiver's partner may take any position they choose on their own sides of the net, on or off the court.

The server alternates serving, first from behind his own right court into the receiver's right service court, then from behind his own left court into the receiver's left service court, and so on. Members of the receiving team alternate receiving service.

If the server serves from behind the wrong court and his mistake is not discovered until the point has been completed, the point stands as played, but thereafter the server must serve from the correct court according to the score. If the server serves from behind the wrong court and the mistake is detected by the receiving team after the service has been delivered and that team does not attempt to return the service, the server loses the point.

The ball served must pass over the net cleanly and hit the deck within the proper service court before the receiver may return it.

Receiver may not volley the serve, *i.e.*, strike the ball before it has bounced. If he does so, receiver loses the point outright.

RULE 8

Delivery of the Service

The service is delivered as follows: the server takes an initial position behind the baseline and between an imaginary extension of the center mark and the sideline, as described in Rule 7. The server then projects the ball by hand into the air in any direction, and before it hits the ground strikes the ball with his paddle. At the moment of impact the service delivery is completed.

> NOTE: The serve may be delivered overhand, underhand or sidearm as the server chooses. There is no obligation on server's part to inform receiver as to his intention, and server may vary his type of delivery.

RULE 9

Only One Service

Only one service is allowed. If the service is a fault, the server loses the point. If the service is a let, the server serves the point again.

RULE 10

Fault or Out

The serve is a fault if:

> (a) the server does not take a legal position as described in Rules 7 and 8;
> (b) the server commits a footfault (see Rule 11);
> (c) the server misses the ball completely in attempting to strike it;
> (d) the ball does not land in the proper service court;
> (e) the ball served hits the server's partner;

(f) the ball touches a court fixture other than the net, band or center strap before it hits the deck. If it touches any of the above fixtures and then lands within the proper service court, it is a let (see Rule 13).

COMMENT: It is customary for the receiving team, especially receiver's partner, to determine whether the serve is a fault by reason of (a) the ball's having landed outside the proper service court or (b) the server's having violated the footfault rule. The first such call of a footfault on each server in a match not being officiated shall be a let. After his "grace fault" it is loss of point.

Under tournament conditions, if there are linesmen, they assume the responsibility for calling all footfaults. At any time in any round of a tournament match any player is entitled to request a footfault judge and/or linesmen.

A *ball* in *play* (other than a serve) is out if it does not land within the court on the proper side of the net after either crossing the net or touching the net, post, cord, band or center strap.

NOTE: Since all parts of the lines bounding the court are deemed to be within the court, a ball that touches any part of a line is good.

The usual procedure is for the receiving team to make line calls on its own side of the net in matches in which there are no linesmen. Any doubts should be resolved in favor of the opponents.

RULE 11

Footfault

The server shall, throughout delivery of the service, up to the moment of impact of paddle and ball:

A. Not change his position by walking or running.

B. Not touch, with either foot, any area other than that behind the baseline within the imaginary extension of the center mark and the sideline.

NOTE: The server shall not by the following movements of his feet be deemed to "change his position by walking or running:"

  i. Slight movements of the feet which do not materially affect the location originally taken by him;

 ii. An unrestricted movement of one foot, so long as the other foot maintains continuously its original contact with the deck;

iii. Leaving the deck with both feet.

RULE 12

Receiving Team Must Be Ready

The server must not deliver his serve until the receiving team is ready. If the receiver makes any attempt to return the ball, he is deemed to be ready. Also, if the receiver attempts to return the ball it is deemed that his partner also is ready.

If the receiver says that he is not ready as a serve is being delivered, the serve shall be played again, provided the receiver does not attempt to return the ball. In such case, the receiver may not claim a fault should the serve land outside the service court.

RULE 13

A Let

In all cases where a let is called, the point is to be replayed.

The *service* is a let if:

(a) it touches the net cord, center strap or band and then lands in the proper service court;

(b) after touching the net, band or center strap it touches either member of the receiving team or anything they are wearing or carrying before hitting the deck, regardless of where they might be standing, on or off the court;

(c) it is delivered when the receiving team is not ready (see Rule 12).

A *ball in play* is a let if:

(d) it hits an overhanging obstruction such as a tree limb or a crossbeam;

(e) the ball becomes broken in the course of a point;

(f) play is interrupted by an accidental occurrence such as a ball from another court bouncing into the court.

NOTE: In any situation during the play of a point when a let may be called, if the player who could call the let does not do so immediately and permits play to continue, that decision is binding on his team. It is not reasonable to opt not to call a let, strike the ball for loss of point, and then ask for a let to be called.

RULE 14

Serve Touching Receiving Team

If the serve touches the receiver or the receiver's partner or anything they are wearing or carrying before the ball has hit the deck, the server wins the point outright, provided the serve is not a let as described in Rule 13(b). This ruling applies whether the member of the receiving team is hit while he is standing on or off the court.

RULE 15

When Receiver Becomes Server

At the end of the first game of a set the receiving team becomes the serving team. The partners decide between them who will serve first in each set. The order of service remains in force for that entire set.

RULE 16

Serving or Receiving Out of Turn

If a player serves out of turn the player who should be serving must take over the serving from the point that the mistake is discovered. All points stand as played.

If an entire game is served by the wrong player the game score stands as played, but the order of service remains as altered, so that in no case may one player on a team serve three games in a row.

If the receiving team receives from the wrong sides of their court (as established in their first receiving game of the set) they must play that entire game from the "wrong courts" but must revert to the original sides of their court the next game they are receivers.

RULE 17

Ball Remains in Play

Once a ball is put into play by service, it remains in play until the point is decided, unless a fault or a let is called.

> EXPLANATION: A player may not catch a ball which appears to be going out of bounds and claim the point. The ball is in play until it actually hits the screen on the fly, or bounces on the deck. A player catching or stopping a ball and calling "out" before the ball is legally out loses the point for his team.

RULE 18

Loss of Point

A team loses the point if:

(a) the ball bounces a second time on its side of the net, provided the first bounce was within the court;

DISCUSSION: Sometimes it is difficult to determine whether a player attempting to retrieve a ball, especially a drop shot, that has bounced and is about to bounce again, actually strikes the ball before it bounces the second time. Propriety dictates that the player attempting to hit the ball is honor bound to call "not up" if he feels the ball did in fact bounce twice. A player who has any doubt in this situation will ask the nearest opponent, after the point has been decided, "was I up?" If the opponent says no, the point should be conceded.

(b) a player returns the ball in such a way that it hits:
 i. the deck on the other side of the net outside the sidelines or baseline;
 ii. any object, other than an opposing player, on the other side of the net outside the sidelines or baseline;
 iii. the net, post, cord, band or center strap and does not then land within the court on the other side of the net.
(c) a player volleys the ball and fails to make a good return, even when standing outside the court:

EXPLANATION: A player standing outside the court volleys at his own risk. It is not proper to volley the ball and simultaneously call it "out," for if the ball is volleyed it is in play.

(d) a player touches or strikes the ball more than

once in making a stroke (commonly called a double hit or "carry");

(e) a player volleys the ball before it has crossed over to his side of the net, i.e. reaches over the net to strike the ball, making contact on the opponents' side of the net; see rule 20(b).

(f) a player is touched by a ball in play, unless it is a let service (see Rule 13b).

NOTE: It does not matter whether the player is inside or outside the court, whether he is hit squarely or his clothing merely grazed, or whether the contact is accidental or purposeful. If a ball touches anything other than a player's paddle it is loss of point.

(g) a player throws his paddle at the ball in play and hits it;

(h) a player bounces the ball over the screen and out of the enclosure or into a lighting fixture, whether or not the ball rebounds back into the court.

(i) a player or anything he wears or carries touches the net, post, cord, band or center strap, or the court surface on the opponents' side of the net, within the boundary lines, while the ball is in play.

NOTE: If the point has already been concluded it is not a violation to touch any of these fixtures. Also, if in rushing to retrieve a drop shot, a player's momentum carries him past the net post onto the opponents' side of the net, this is not loss of point unless the player actually steps inside the opponents' court or interferes with one of the opponents. Mere physical contact with an opponent is not loss of point unless such contact hinders the opponent.
When a player is standing at the net and the opponent hits the ball into the net in such a way that it pushes the net against his paddle or his person, the net player

loses the point. It does not matter that the ball was not going over the net. The net player loses the point because he made contact with the net while the ball was was still in play.

RULE 19

Ball Touching Court Fixtures

If the ball in play touches a court fixture (as defined in Rule 2) after it has hit the deck within the boundaries of the court, the ball remains in play and may be returned, so long as it has not hit the deck a second time on the same side of the net.

EXCEPTIONS: If the ball hits a lighting fixture, the point is concluded—loss of point for striker. If the ball hits a crossbeam it is a let.

In matches in which an umpire and an umpire's chair are inside the enclosure, a ball striking either the umpire or his chair prior to landing in the opponents' court is loss of point for the striker.

RULE 20

Good Return

It is a good return if:

(a) the ball touches the net, posts, cord, band or center strap and then hits the deck within the proper court;

(b) the ball, served or returned, hits the deck within the proper court and rebounds or is blown back over the net, and the player whose turn it is to strike reaches over the net and plays the ball, provided that neither he nor any part of his clothing or equipment touches the net, posts, cord, band or center strap or the deck within his opponents' court, and that the stroke is otherwise good. (See also Rule 21: Interference.)

(c) the ball is returned outside the post, either above or below the level of the top of the net, whether or not it touches the post, provided that it then hits the deck within the proper court.

NOTE: It is not a good return if the ball is hit through the open space between the net and the post.

(d) a player's paddle passes over the net after he has returned the ball, provided that the ball had crossed to his side of the net before being struck by him, and that the stroke is otherwise good.

RULE 21

Interference

In case a player is hindered in making a stroke by anything not within his control, the point is replayed.

CLARIFICATION: If a tree branch or a ball from another court should interfere with play, a let should be called immediately. However, if a player bumps into his own partner or is interfered with by a court fixture, that is not grounds for a let.

In the situation covered by Rule 20(b), if the player who is attempting to strike the ball is willfully hindered by his opponent, the player is entitled to the point by reason of interference, whether such interference is verbal or physical. However, if it is agreed that such interference was unintentional, a let should be called.

RULE 22

Scoring

(a) The Game:

The first point is called 15, although it is also commonly called 5.
The second point is called 30.
The third point is called 40.
The fourth point is Game.

When both teams score 15, or both score 30, the score is called "15 all" or "30 all."

When both teams score 40, the score is called Deuce. The next point after Deuce is called Advantage for the team winning it, thus Advantage Server (or more usually Ad In), if the serving team wins, and Advantage Receiver (or Ad Out), if the receiving team wins. If the team with the Advantage wins the next point, it wins the game. If the other team wins that point, the score reverts to Deuce. This continues indefinitely until one or the other team wins two points in a row from deuce, which wins the game. Zero or no points is called Love. A game that is won "at love" means that the losing team scored no points.

(b) The Set:

The team which first wins 6 games wins the Set.

However, the winning team must have a margin of 2 games, and a set played under the traditional rules continues until one team has such a 2-game margin, e.g. 8-6 or 11-9.

A set that is won "at love" means that the losing team scored no games.

Should the players or the tournament committee decide to play a Tiebreak, a special procedure is followed when the game score is 6 all. (See Appendix C.)

The APTA recommends the use of the 12-point Tiebreak, especially when time is a problem. Tournament committees should announce in the tournament rules whether the Tiebreak is to be played.

(c) The Match:

Customarily a match is best of 3 sets but a tournament committee has the right to require best of 5 in the late rounds or the finals of a Men's Tournament.

COMMENT: In matches played without an umpire

the server should announce the point scores as the game goes on, and the game score at the end of his service game. Misunderstandings will be averted if this practice is followed.

RECOMMENDED NUMBER OF SETS TO BE PLAYED IN DIFFERENT EVENTS

Junior Girls—Ages 18 and 15

> 2 out of 3 all through the tournament

Junior Boys—Age 15

> 2 out of 3 all through the tournament

Junior Boys—Age 18

> 2 out of 3 to the finals
> 3 out of 5 finals

Men's—Ranking Tournaments

> 2 out of 3 to the finals
> 3 out of 5 finals

Men's—National

> 2 out of 3 to quarters,
> then 3 out of 5

Men's—45

> 2 out of 3 to finals
> finals—3 out of 5

Men's—Seniors

> 2 out of 3 all the way

Men's—Veterans

> 2 out of 3 all the way

Ladies'

> 2 out of 3 all the way

Mixed

> 2 out of 3 all the way

RULE 23

When Teams Change Sides

Teams change sides at the end of the first, third, fifth and every subsequent odd-numbered game of each set.

When a set ends on an odd total of games, e.g. 6-3, the teams "change for one"—that is, they change sides for one game, and then change sides again after the first game of the next set. When the set ends on an even total of games, e.g. 6-4, the teams "stay for one" and then change sides after the first game of the next set.

RULE 24

Continuous Play

Play shall be continuous from the first serve of the first game until the conclusion of the match, except:

(a) for rest periods permitted by tournament officials;

(b) when changing sides on the odd games, a maximum of one minute is allowed for players to towel off, change equipment, rest, etc.

(c) Play shall never be suspended, delayed or interfered with for the purpose of enabling a player to recover his strength or to receive instruction or advice. The umpire shall be the sole judge of such suspension, delay or interference, and after giving due warning he may disqualify the offender. No allowance may be made for natural loss of physical condition such as cramps, faintness or loss of wind. Consideration may be given by the umpire for accidental loss of physical ability or condition.

NOTE 1: In the event of an accident, a fall, collision with a net post, a sprained ankle, and the like, up to a ten-minute suspension in play may be authorized. A default will be mandatory if play is not resumed immediately after the suspension.

NOTE 2: If a player's clothing, footwear, or equipment becomes out of adjustment in such a way that it is impossible or undesirable for him to play on, the provisions in Note 1 shall apply.

CLARIFICATION: The intent of the Continuous Play Rule is to prevent unauthorized rest periods for players who are tired and to discourage stalling tactics for whatever purpose. In the event of an accident, the umpire or tournament chairman shall consider a temporary suspension of play.

If a match is adjourned for a legitimate reason, e.g. a sudden rainstorm, when the match is resumed (a) the teams are entitled to a full warmup and (b) the match must begin precisely where it left off, with the same game and point score, same server, same sides of the court, and same order of service.

RULE 25

Only One Hit

In the course of making a return, only one player may hit the ball. If both players, either simultaneously or consecutively, hit the ball, it is an illegal return and loss of point. Mere clashing of paddles does not constitute an illegal return, provided that only one player strikes the ball.

RULE 26

Balls off Screens

If a ball in play or on the serve hits the deck in the proper court and then touches any part of the back or side screens, or both screens, or the horizontal top rails, or the snow boards, it may be played, so long as it does not bounce on the deck a second time on the same side of the net before being hit by the player.

NOTE: A ball taken off the screen must be returned directly over the net into the opponents' court. It may not be caromed back indirectly by being hit from paddle to screen and thence into the opponents' court.

APPENDIX A

BALL PERFORMANCE STANDARDS AND ACCEPTABLE TOLERANCES

The APTA has established the following Performance Standards and Acceptable Tolerances for ball.

The APTA reserves the right to withhold or terminate approval if the Association feels the Standards have not been met by a manufacturer, and to approve balls for sanctioned play as it sees fit.

I. Bounce Test for Rebound

Balls conditioned at 70 degrees F. for 24 hours, then dropped from 90 inches to a concrete slab, and the rebound measured. Bounce to be measured from bottom of ball.

Rebound

Acceptable tolerance

43″ thru 48″

II. Weight Test

Acceptable tolerance

70 gms. thru 75 gms.

III. Diameter Test

Measure diameter along two perpendicular axes of the ball. Both readings must be within tolerance.

	Standard	Acceptable tolerance
Diameter	$2\frac{1}{2}$ ″	$2\frac{1}{2}″\pm\frac{1}{32}″$

APPENDIX B

PLATFORM TENNIS PADDLE STANDARDS AND ACCEPTABLE TOLERANCES

	Standard	Tolerance
Total Length	17″ maximum	none
Thickness (including rim)	⅜″ ± ¹⁄₁₆″	
Handle Length	6⅝″ maximum	none
Width of Head (at widest point)	8¼″ maximum	
Play Length (handle to outside edge of rim	10⅜″ maximum	
Bolts and Nuts	flat and flush (Preferably concealed by grip)	none
Holes—Number	87 maximum	
Holes—Diameter	⅜″	none
Edges—Shape	Squared or rounded	none
Surface Finish	Smooth	none
Surface	Flat	none

APPENDIX C

THE APTA APPROVED 12-POINT TIEBREAK FOR PLATFORM TENNIS
REVISED 12-POINT TIEBREAKER

At six games all the players continue to serve in order and from the same side as before. *The server of the first point of the tie-breaker will serve only one point and that to the Ad Court.* Each player will then, in normal service rotation, serve twice; first to the Deuce Court, then to the Ad Court. The single point served by the initial server of the tiebreaker results in an immediate change of sides and teams will continue to change sides in the normal pattern as if the server had served an entire game. First team to win 7 points wins set, although if it be 6 points all, the team must win by 2 points in a row. The set shall be scored at 7-6. The team receiving service for the first point of the tie-breaker shall begin serving the next set from the opposite side from which it received the first point. The teams shall change sides after the first game.

Example

North

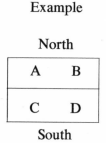

South

A started serving the set from N Side.

It's 6 games all and it's A's turn to serve again.

1) A serves *once* (Ad Court) from N side.

Change Sides

2) C serves twice from N side.*

(Deuce Court first; Ad Court second)

3) B serves twice from S side.

(Deuce Court first; Ad Court second)

Change Sides

4) D serves twice from S Side.

(Deuce Court first; Ad Court second)

5) A serves twice from N side.

(Deuce Court first; Ad Court second)

Change sides and repeat this order until one
team reaches 7 points or wins by 2 points after
each team reaches 6 points.

6) Team C-D starts serving next set from N side.

7) Teams change sides after 1 game.

*Assuming that C has been following A in service order.

THE DETERMINING SET OF THE FINAL ROUND OF
EACH TOURNAMENT MUST BE PLAYED OUT WITH-
OUT A TIEBREAKER (THIRD SET OF 2-OUT-OF-3-SET
MATCH, AND FIFTH SET OF 3-OUT-OF-5-SET MATCH).

If a ball change is called for on a tiebreaker game, the change
should be deferred until the second game of the following set, to
preserve the alternation of the right to serve first with the new
ball.

i

Catalog

If you are interested in a list of fine Paperback
books, covering a wide range of subjects
and interests, send your name and address,
requesting your free catalog, to:

McGraw-Hill Paperbacks
1221 Avenue of Americas
New York, N.Y. 10020

Sports

HOW TO PLAY PLATFORM TENNIS

Fourth Revised Edition

Dick Squires

Platform tennis appeals to increasing numbers of men and women for many reasons: it's easy to learn yet difficult to master, it's a year-round outdoor sport for virtually any kind of weather, and it improves one's tennis game. Furthermore, courts occupy just one-fourth of the space of tennis courts and can be built on practically any terrain.

Dick Squires, one of the country's most versatile racquet-wielders, here articulately describes the fundamentals of this sport. He provides instruction on basic strokes, shotmaking, strategy and equipment. Full-page action photographs of today's leading players as well as line drawings illustrate the text. Though he writes for the beginner who wants to learn the proper way, he has a great deal of useful advice for the experienced player as well.

Dick Squires has competed in tennis, squash racquets, squash tennis and platform tennis on national and international levels and has held U.S. titles in three of these sports. He is founder and president of U.S. Platform Tennis Clubs; vice-president of E. L. Wagner Co., Inc., paddle court builders; a member of The PRO-Keds Sports Advisory Staff; and a consultant to General Sportcraft Co. Ltd.

McGraw-Hill Paperbacks   0-07-060530-0